George Castrio
1468-2018

550 Years from the Death of the
National Hero of the Albanian People
and Great Defender of European Civilization

George Castriota Scanderbeg

George Castriota Scanderbeg

SCANDERBEG

A History of George Castriota
and the Albanian Resistance
to Islamic Expansion
in Fifteenth Century Europe

A.K. Brackob

HISTRIA
Buffalo ◊ Las Vegas ◊ Palm Beach

Published in the United States of America by Histria LLC
HistriaBooks.com

Library of Congress Control Number: 2018902272

ISBN 978-1-59211-003-2 (hardcover)
ISBN 978-1-59211-000-1 (paperback)
ISBN 978-1-59211-005-6 (ebook)

In memory of
Academician Cornelia Bodea,
friend and scholar

Prologue

"There is an abundance of military knowledge to be picked out of the lives of Gustav Adolphus and Charles XII, King of Sweden, and of Zisca the Bohemian; and if a tolerable account could be got of the exploits of Scanderbeg, it would be inestimable; for he excels all the officers, ancient and modern, in the conduct of a small defensive army. I met with him in the Turkish History, but nowhere else."

— James Wolfe to Thomas Townshend, 18 July 1756[1]

The struggle led by George Castriota Scanderbeg to defend Europe against the Islamic onslaught of the Ottoman Turks has been much celebrated. For a quarter of a century, from 1443 until his death in 1468, he used his military prowess to thwart the efforts of the most powerful Empire in the world at that time to subdue his tiny country. Despite this, few English language studies of his remarkable feat have been written. The British General of French and Indian War fame, James Wolfe's comment on Scanderbeg recognizes the historical importance of the Albanian resistance to the Ottomans in the fifteenth century, but since his complaint, over

---

[1]"Lt. Col. James Wolfe to Thomas Townshend, Devises, Sunday, 18 July 1756" in Willson, *The Life and Letters of James Wolfe*, p. 296.

two and a half centuries ago, that he could only find mention of Scanderbeg in Richard Knolles' *The Generall Historie of the Turkes*, relatively few works on the subject have appeared in major languages.

In the over five hundred years that have passed since Scanderbeg's cavalry roamed the mountains of Albania, the struggle he led has been viewed in many different ways. The remarkable nature of his achievement has led many to view it as an almost miraculous feat. Writing of Scanderbeg in 1905, William J. Armstrong said, "the exploits even of the renowned paladins of the crusades, whether Godfrey or Tancred or Richard or Raymond, pale to insignificance by similar comparison. Only the legendary feats of King Arthur and his knights, or of the Guardsmen of Dumas suggest a parallel of wondrous achievement."[2]

Though not all writers have accorded to Scanderbeg the same type of mythical glorification bestowed upon him by Armstrong, historians have generally portrayed him as a Christian hero *par excellence*. During his lifetime, Europe viewed him as the leader in the holy struggle to defend Christendom from the onslaught of the Islamic invaders; Pope Calixtus III wrote to the Albanian leader: "We have always felt that because of your outstanding efforts and memorable victories you have, above all other Catholic rulers, served the Christian faith and the Church." Pope Pius II

---

[2]Armstrong, *The Heroes of Defeat*, p. 187.

regarded him as the spearhead of his efforts to organize a great anti-Ottoman crusade.

His legacy has even inspired efforts by the Catholic Church to canonize him. He has retained an image similar to Saint George or the Archangel Michael, a militant fighter for Christendom, the leader of a holy crusade against the Turkish Infidels. To commemorate the 500th anniversary of Scanderbeg's death, in 1968, Pope Paul VI declared: "This Holy See is pleased to join in the praise of this man of great nobility, a faithful son of the Church and a son whom sovereign pontiffs before us have praised possibly more glowingly than any other man of his time. For twenty-five years, he saved his country from the assault of enemies. He defended his country threatened by the greatest danger, at the head of an army which the rampart and defense of Christianity."[3]

The image of Scanderbeg took additional significance with the rise national movement in Albania during the nineteenth and twentieth centuries. Scanderbeg assumed the role of a national hero. The Albanian Orthodox Bishop and historian Fan Noli clearly expressed this sentiment, writing: "In 1912 Ismail Kemal raised the flag of Scanderbeg in Valona when he declared Albanian independence. Scanderbeg was our inspiration in those first arduous years during the birth pangs and growing pains of Albania. He has inspired our poets, historians, and sculptors. And he still inspires us.

---

[3]Pope Paul VI in *Gjergj Kastrioti Skenderbeu*, 1468-1968, p. 184.

P.T   GIORGIO CASTRIOTTO
SCANDERBECH

Sometimes I wonder whether there is any other living man who is alive today as he is!"[4]

Yet to understand the man and the movement he led it is necessary to go beyond the constraints of nationalism and religious or political ideology. It is essential not only to understand the external factors affecting the Albanian resistance, namely Ottoman and Venetian imperialism, but to analyze its internal dynamics as well. To do this, it must be considered in light of the political, social, and economic crisis which occurred throughout Europe during the fourteenth and fifteenth centuries as Islam encroached upon the continent and the peoples of southeastern Europe bore the brunt of the struggle to defend Christianity. Only in this way can the historical significance of Scanderbeg's accomplishments be fully appreciated, and the successes and failures of the Albanian resistance understood.

As the 550th anniversary of the death of the great Albanian leader is commemorated in 2018, Scanderbeg remains as relevant as ever. One of the true heroes of the Middle Ages, it is unfortunate that his remarkable story remains little known outside of Albania. He defended Europe for a quarter of a century and, it can rightly be said, helped to save Western Civilization from being overrun by Islam. Although the challenges have changed over the centuries, the

---

[4]Fan Noli, "Problems on the Biographical Literature on Skenderbeg," in *Gjergj Kastrioti-Skenderbeu*, p. 203. On the significance of Scanderbeg in the Albanian national movement, see also, Treptow, *From Zalmoxis to Jan Palach*, pp. 91-93.

clash of civilizations, which the history of the Albanian struggle to fend off the Islamic onslaught represents, continues today. The failures of the West to understand the threat and to organize effectively to defend against it has remained a persistent problem throughout the centuries. As a result, it is all the more worth noting the contribution that this tiny land, led by George Castriota, made in the fight to preserve Western civilization.

The Albanian people paid a heavy price for the failure of Europe to act decisively to defend its culture and civilization from the Islamic threat. Despite hardships, however, Albanians harmonize these great civilizations. The people, largely abandoned by the powers of Europe, maintained their unique identity and brought harmony to their land through the strength of their culture. As we commemorate this important anniversary, this book aims to draw attention to the genius and remarkable achievements of Scanderbeg and the Albanian people and to mark the important contribution they have made to European civilization.

A.K. Brackob

Chapter 1
The Albanian Background

"Morn dawns; and with it stern Albania's hills,
Dark Suli's rocks, and Pindus' inland peak,
Robed half in mist, bedewed with snowy rills,
Arrayed in many a dun and purple streak,
Arise, and, as the clouds along them break,
Disclose the dwelling of the mountaineer;
Here roams the wolf, the eagle whets his beak,
Birds, beasts of prey, and wilder men appear,
And gathering storms convulse the closing year."

— Lord Byron, Childe Harold's Pilgrimage[5]

Albania has always been a land of mystery. Though it shares a common border with Greece and is within fifty miles of the Italian peninsula, across the strait of Otranto, it remains, as the renowned historian Edward Gibbon once said, "the remotest part of Europe." This is in large part due to its rugged mountains which have protected their inhabitants from invaders, while at the same time isolating them from the outside world. It is this isolation and the close ties to nature and the land which, as Byron's verses demon-

---

[5]Lord Byron, *Childe Harold's Pilgrimage*, p. 66 [Canto II, XVII].

strate, have made it seem such a fascinating place. This setting has no doubt contributed to the legendary status of
George Castriota Scanderbeg.

The coastal plain of Albania ranges from five to twenty-
five miles wide. From the shore of the Adriatic it rises gradually to a little over one hundred feet above sea level. The
elevation rises rapidly at the edge of the coastal plain, with
shrub predominating in the area between six hundred and
sixteen hundred feet above sea level. The mountains which
dominate the land rise from the edge of the coastal plain to
as high as eight thousand feet above sea level. Most villages
are located in the middle region, between sixteen hundred
and three thousand feet, which offers both the security of
the mountains and some of the most fertile land. Immense
forests covered the mountain regions as high as seven thousand feet in the fifteenth century. The principal agricultural
crop grown in this area during this time was wheat, while
the leaves from the oak trees common in these elevations
were used to feed livestock. In the higher elevations, pine
trees predominated. Though the land in this zone is of little
value for raising crops, the grass is excellent for summer
grazing. Numerous valleys, narrow and steep sided, are a
common feature of northern and central Albania, while in
the southern part of the country there are few valleys, except for deep ravines with rivers on their floors. Because of
their high gradients and pronounced L-shaped bends the
rivers of Albania are for the most part unnavigable, assuring
difficult access to the interior. In contrast to the mild climate

of the coastal region, the mountain climate is harsh and the weather is prone to sudden and dramatic changes, especially in the winter months when blizzards and heavy snowfall make transportation extremely difficult. Rainfall is heavy, particularly during March and November when heavy precipitation in the higher elevations often causes flooding in the coastal plains.

Geography played an important role in the success of Scanderbeg's resistance to the Ottomans. The mountains served as a natural shield against the Islamic invaders; in his History of Mehmed the Conqueror, the Greek chronicler Kritoboulos, a contemporary of these events, testified to this fact: "there were but one or two passes through the mountains into the country, they guarded these with strong garrisons, and kept their land inviolate from enemies, and free from injury, unless a large force should invade it and forcibly occupy the mountains and the passes, and so open a door into the whole country."[6]

Strongholds such as Sfietgrade, an important fortress protecting the passes into the interior, were built in the rugged mountains, providing difficult access and making it impossible for attackers to plant their cannons with any effect. Likewise, Scanderbeg's capital of Croya [Krujë in Albanian], which withstood determined sieges by both Murad II and Mehmed the Conqueror, was situated in the heavily for-

---

[6]Kritovoulos, *History of Mehmed the Conqueror*, p. 211 (V,64).

ested mountains near the coastal plain, making it almost impregnable. By exploiting the difficult geography of northern and central Albania, Scanderbeg overcame the disparity of forces he regularly faced when fighting the Ottomans.

✳✳✳

The Albanians are direct descendants of the ancient Illyrians who inhabited the Balkan peninsula since pre-Homeric times. The Illyrians were renowned as great warriors leading the Greek historian Thucydides to comment that they "are a race of fighters," feared by the Greeks.[7] This martial spirit remains an essential part of the Albanian character, even in the fifteenth century. Scanderbeg himself wrote to the Prince of Taranto, with whom he was in conflict, recalling the noble heritage of his people: "Our ancestors were Epirotes, of whom came that Pyrrhus whose attack the Romans could hardly resist, who took by force of arms Tarentum and many other Italian towns. You cannot set against the valiant Epirotes the Tarentines, a sodden race born to catch fish. If you say that Albania is part of Macedonia, you concede to us far nobler ancestors, who penetrated with Alexander into India, laying low with incredible success all the nations between who opposed them."[8]

Both geography and politics have made the Albanians a warlike people; the land has always been a frontier area,

---

[7]Thucydides, *The Peloponnesian War*, p. 340.

[8]Pius II, "The Commentaries of Pius II, Books VI-IX," p. 460.

between Byzantium and Rome, Orthodoxy and Catholicism, then between Christianity and Islam, and most recently between Communism and the Free World, and its mountains always formed a symbolic barrier. It is, in fact, these mountains that allowed the Albanians to preserve their ethnic identity in face of the Slavic invasions in the early Middle Ages. Their distinct language, an offspring of ancient Illyrian, has been another important factor in maintaining the ethnic unity of the people.

The uniqueness of their language and culture, preserved by their geographic isolation, has made the Albanians always aware of their ethnic individuality. John Cam Hobhouse, who accompanied Lord Byron during his travels in Albania early in the nineteenth century, wrote, "Nationality, a passion at all times stronger in mountaineers than in inhabitants of the plains, is most conspicuous in their character."[9] Despite religious differences and the mountains which not only kept foreigners out, but also divided people of different regions from one another, Albanians were at all times aware of themselves as a separate ethnic group, distinct from their Slavic and Greek neighbors.

The geographic isolation of Albania helped to preserve a relatively ethnically homogeneous society, which helped to strengthen the sense of nationality observed by Hobhouse. In the fifteenth century, the chief unit of organization

---

[9]Hobhouse, *A Journey through Albania*, p. 148.

was the local village. The village was essentially an extended family, similar to the Slavic *zadruga*; several brothers, or even first cousins, lived together in the peasant household. Because of these close ties, marriage between two people of the same village, whether related or not, was forbidden as incestuous. Brides were brought in from other villages in the region.

The family ties, whether by marriage, blood or adoption, extended beyond the boundaries of the village to neighboring communities. These ties, no doubt expanded by marriage, created a system of tribal organization in which a particular family assumed the role of political leader and protector of the region.

This system of organization created greater possibilities for defense, making it easier to raise armies, while assuring the distribution of labor to meet the needs of the local community. It also created the basis of a type of feudal organization, as local communities were obligated to provide labor or goods to the ruling family in return for the social order and protection which it provided. Thus, the origins of a distinct Albanian feudalism can be found in the extension of these familial ties and the need to organize to ensure social order and defense.

The Albanian nobility, up to the Ottoman conquest, developed almost exclusively from the peasantry itself, and played an important and necessary function in medieval society. Customary laws, usually administered by these tribal leaders, governed the relationships between people. Two of the mountain legal codes which survived to the twentieth century are the *Code of Scanderbeg* and the *Code of Lekë Dukagjin*, named after an older contemporary of the Albanian hero.[10] A principal common to both legal codes is equality before the law, a reflection of the individualism characteristic of this mountain people.

***

Christianity appeared in Albania during the second century A.D., making its initial impact in the coastal cities of Durazzo [Durrës in Albanian] and Valona [Vlorë in Albanian], brought there by travelers and sailors who passed through these important ports of the Roman province of Illyria.

Over the centuries, Christianity gradually made its way inland, being imposed upon pre-existing beliefs. Albania marked the frontier between the Eastern Orthodox and Roman Catholic Churches. Originally it was under the jurisdiction of the Roman Church, but during the War of Images, which resulted from the iconoclastic controversy, a dispute over the veneration of icons in the Church, in 726, the Byzantine Emperor Leo III placed Albania, along with Crete, Sicily, and Calabria, under the control of the Patriarch of Constantinople. The conflicts within the Church, leading to the Great Schism in 1054, left a permanent mark on the

---

[10]The Code of Leke Dukagjin is published in a bilingual edition, *Kanuni i Leke Dukagjinit/The Code of Leke Dukagjini.*

country. By the fifteenth century, the country was religiously divided; the south predominantly Orthodox, while the north was mainly Catholic.

Despite the competing interests of the Eastern and Western Churches, the religious practices of the vast majority of Albanians differed very little. In 1439, the Council of Florence briefly resolved the division between the two principal branches of Christianity by uniting the Orthodox and Catholic churches. In a supreme effort to unite Christendom in face of the Islamic threat, the Union called for acceptance of four main theological points as the basis for healing the Great Schism: 1) acceptance of Papal supremacy; 2) the use of unleavened bread for the sacrament of the Eucharist; 3) the acceptance of the Catholic version of the Nicean creed whereby the Holy Spirit is said to proceed from the Father "and the Son"; and 4) acceptance of the doctrine regarding the existence of purgatory. The Byzantines accepted these terms as the basis for the reunification of the Eastern and Western Churches in hopes of securing political and military assistance from the West to stave off an imminent Ottoman conquest. The Union, however, was widely denounced in the Orthodox world which could not let go of its hatred of Rome, despite the imminent threat posed by Islam. Mehmed II's conquest of Constantinople in 1453 dealt the Union of Florence its death blow; the Sultan appointed George Scholarios, a vehement opponent of any reconciliation between the two Christian Churches, as Patriarch of Constantinople.

Despite its failure to resolve the divide between the Eastern and Western branches of Christianity, Scanderbeg's revolt benefitted from the effort at Florence to bring the two Churches together. The Albanians of northern and central Albania were either Catholic or Orthodox and both adhered to the Union established by the Council of Florence only four years before Scanderbeg raised his flag over Croya and proclaimed his lands free of Ottoman domination. The limited interest in organized religion among the mountain people made the divisions among Christians easier to overcome than in other regions of Europe and the Union of Florence had a longer life here as a result. Henry Swinburne, a British traveler to Sicily in the 1770s, remarked that many of the Albanians living there, who had migrated after the Ottoman invasion, still observed the Greek rite, while still adhering to the Union.[11]

Though the population of Albania was almost entirely Christian in the early fifteenth century, Islam made steady inroads as the Ottomans extended their conquests in Southeastern Europe. The process of Islamization began with Christian *timar* holders who had manage to keep possession of their lands by acknowledging the suzerainty of the Sultan. The upper classes of Ottoman society assimilated these Christian *timar* holder who sought favor with the Porte and usually adopted Islam within two generations. Still, adher-

---

[11]Swinburne, *Travels in the Two Sicilies*, vol. I, p. 352.

ence to their new faith was superficial at best. In the late fifteenth and early sixteenth centuries, Albanian chronicler Marin Barletti explained, "[the Albanians] were always more inclined to arms than to religion."[12]

Islam also spread among the population at large. Owing to their geographic isolation, the Albanians were nominal Christians at best, and had little aversion to converting to Islam for political advantages and to avoid paying taxes. Albanians never were religious zealots, instead they adapted to the situations in which they found themselves. Traveling in Albania in the 1820s, the Reverend T.S. Hughes remarked, "the Albanian Mahometan is not more observant of doctrines, rites, and ceremonies under his new law than he was under his old one, and is looked upon with great contempt by the rigid Osmanli. He frequently takes a Christian woman to his wife, carries his sons to mosque, and allows his daughters to attend their mother to church; nay, he even goes himself alternately to both places of worship, and eats with his family out of the same dish, in which are viands forbidden to the disciples of Mahomet."[13] Likewise, Ismail Kemal, the Albanian patriot who hoisted the flag of Scanderbeg to proclaim the independence of his country in Vlora in 1912, wrote, "they make no distinction among

---

[12]Moore, *George Castriot*, p. 60.

[13] Hughes, *Travels in Greece and Albania*, vol. 2, p. 105.

themselves on account of their faith, nor do any of the population arrogate to themselves on these points any superiority or privilege."[14]

The principal Islamic force in Albania was the Bektashi Order of Dervishes, a Moslem pantheistic order highly adaptable to the primitive Christianity practiced in the mountains of Albania. The Bektashi Order achieved success in Albania by imposing Islam on pre-existing Christian beliefs, including the adoption of Christian saints. The doctrinal flexibility of the Bektashi sect promoted the spread of Islam and by the twentieth century Albania was the only nation in Europe with a Muslim majority, with 70% of the population officially adhering to the Islamic faith.

Over the centuries, organized religion played a limited role in the lives of most Albanians. The nineteenth century Albanian nationalist Wassa Effendi [aka Pashko Vasa] noted the limited influence of religion in fundamentally altering Albanian customs, giving an example: "Independently of so many other religious practices which are related to the ancient cult of Pelasges and which neither Christ nor Mahomet have made completely disappear from the minds of the Albanian people, there is the oath on the stone which still exists and is still used in all the mountains of Albania."[15] Likewise, early in the twentieth century Fan Noli

---

[14] Kemal, *The Memoirs of Ismail Kemal Bey*, p. 362.

[15] Effendi, *Etudes sur l'Albanie et les Albanais*, p. 31. The oath on the stone refers to an oath taken when fixing property boundaries.

remarked: "even with a Moslem majority in the population, one with difficulty would be able to find a civilized country... where religious tolerance reigned, becoming even indifference, as in Albania."[16]

The religious history of the Albanians clearly demonstrates that it is a mistake to attribute purely religious motivations to the Albanians who resisted Ottoman expansion into their lands in the fifteenth century. Scanderbeg and his followers were not crusaders, even if fifteenth century Europe perceived them in this way. In the tradition of their ancestors, they fought to preserve their culture, independence, and protect their homes and families. Even though he wrote at the beginning of the nineteenth century, the characterization of the Albanian spirit made by John Cam Hobhouse is equally valid as a description of the principal motivation of Scanderbeg and his followers: "There is a spirit of independence and a love of country, in the whole people, that, in great measure, does away with the vast distinction, observable in other parts of Turkey, between the followers of the two religions. For when natives of other provinces, upon being asked who they are, will say, 'we are Turks' or 'we are

---

[16]Interview with Fan Noli in the Greek newspaper *Politia* in Geneva, 9 September 1924, in Central State Archives of Albania, Tirana, Fund no. 251, Folder 25. I would like to thank Albanian historian Stefanaq Pollo for this reference.

Christians,' a man of this country answers, 'I am an Albanian.'"[17]

The Albanians of the fifteenth century were not nationalists; such a thing did not yet exist. They did, however, possess a sense of ethnic and cultural unity as manifested in their distinct language and culture, which proved to be of great help in organizing a resistance to foreign invaders. Neither cross nor crescent could supplant this ethnic spirit.

***

Feudalism in Albania was of mixed origins. Undoubtedly, its earliest forms can be attributed to the extension of the familial and village system driven by the need for defense and social order in a region. This system extended itself over time until a full-fledged tribal-feudal system emerged, especially in the lower and middle elevations where the need for defense was greater as they were less isolated and the soil was more productive. The productivity of the land allowed a surplus to be produced; an essential condition for social differentiation to develop.

Feudalism grew more rapidly at the beginning of the twelfth century when crusaders, on their way to the Holy Land, carved out fiefs for themselves as they passed

---

[17]Hobhouse, A Journey through Albania, pp. 147-148. Hobhouse's observation is especially valuable because it was made before the beginnings of any sort of national movement among the Albanians. Thus, it is a reflection of their ethnic spirit and not evidence of nationalism in the modern sense of the word.

through parts of Albania. By the fourteenth and fifteenth centuries a full-fledged native aristocracy had developed and a feudal economy existed in the coastal regions, interior plains, and valleys. This process was accelerated by the incorporation of Albania into the Serbian Empire of Stefan Dušan, which, as can be seen reflected in the law code of the Serbian Tsar,[18] was a feudal state.

Following the collapse of the Serbian Empire after Dušan's death in 1355, a process of centralization began among the native feudal aristocracy, again prompted by external threats, as during the second half of that century both the Ottomans and the Venetians sought to establish their control over Albania. Thus, already in the fourteenth century, a sort of feudal crisis beset Albania. The land was torn between this process of centralization among the native aristocracy and the interference of two powerful foreign states who tried to impede this development. This process of centralization was spurred on by greater needs for defense, not only necessary because of the changing technology of warfare and the increasing size of armies, but also because Albania was now becoming a frontier land in the great struggle between Christianity and Islam. In fact, long before this time, Albania had been a borderland between the Byzantine East and the Catholic West. It was a key outpost of the Byzantine Emperors and of great strategic importance as it represented the best point of access along the Adriatic coast to

---

[18]See "The Code of Stephan Dušan," parts I and II.

the heart of the Eastern Empire. This had been true even in ancient times when the Via Egnatia continued the Via Appia, placing Albania on the principal road from Rome to Greece.

The Byzantine Emperors took great care to assure that Albania would remain firmly under the control of their Empire. As the French historian Alain Ducellier explained, "Albania, beginning with the early Byzantine Epoch, became an imposing fortified complex, carefully and constantly maintained... to hold on to Albania was a matter of life and death for the Empire. One can understand why there was no question of letting Albania become a hostile political entity or even an autonomy."[19]

The special status of Albania as a frontier outpost and its strategic importance combined to prevent the formation of centralized state on the territory of medieval Albania. While the sort of feudal system I have described developed in the lower and middle elevations, communities of free peasants survived in the mountain regions. In these communities, women attended to the household affairs and worked in the fields, usually not very large due to the marginal nature of the land, while the men tended their flocks of sheep in the highlands. These tended to be self-sufficient units in which artisans and craftsmen were drawn from the

---

[19]Ducellier, "Genesis and Failure of the Albanian State," p. 6.

peasant ranks, as was common throughout most of Europe.[20] These communities were also organized on a tribal basis, but on a very local level, as the geographic conditions ruled out the need for the development of a feudal aristocracy.

Flourishing cities dotted the coastline of Albania during the fourteenth and fifteenth centuries. The major ports were Durazzo, which had been an important harbor since its founding in the seventh century B.C., and Valona, the principal port in the southern part of the country. These coastal cities had a developing middle class whose prosperity depended largely upon Venetian trade with the interior. Ever since the Fourth Crusade at the beginning of the thirteenth century, Venice had sought to gain control over the coastline to exploit the rich economic resources of Albania. The nobility sent wheat, the principal agricultural product of the country during this time, via the rivers and overland to the coastal cities where it was sold to foreign merchants. Already in the thirteenth century Albania had become an important wheat exporter to Venice, Ragusa, and Constantinople meaning that the country was producing a significant surplus of grain.

During the fourteenth century, the Venetians used their sea power to exclude other foreign merchants from the Albanian coastal wheat trade. Interested mainly in the economic exploitation of the country, the Venetians did not

---

[20]Hilton, *Bond Men Made Free*, p. 37.

seek direct political control over the coast, which would have been costly and difficult to maintain. Instead, they formed alliances with nobles who agreed to supply their agricultural goods exclusively to Venice, at fixed prices, thereby excluding other foreign merchants from the Albanian grain trade. This was, in fact, the traditional policy followed by the Republic of St. Mark in areas where it had a direct economic interest. The growing threat posed by the Ottomans, however, finally led Venice to seize control of Durazzo in 1392, and most other major coastal cities of northern and central Albania the following year. Venetian administration was established in these cities, and commerce was placed solely in the hands of Venetian merchants, thus destroying the native merchant class, while at the same time enslaving numerous Albanians to serve as oarsmen in their fleet.

Venetian rule imposed heavy taxes and labor obligations upon the peasants in the coastal areas leading to major uprisings in 1399 and 1405. The causes of these rebellions lie in the fact that Venetian administration upset the traditional relations between the peasants and the native nobility. Thus, the peasants must be seen as a conservative force, instead of a revolutionary group. The Venetian economic monopoly extended to include other commodities in addition to wheat, such as wool, cheese, salt, and wood and pine pitch used for shipbuilding. In opposition to the trend toward the centralization of aristocratic power, the Republic

of St. Mark sought to maintain fragmentation among the nobility so that no local power could arise strong enough to
break the Venetian monopoly over Albanian economic resources.

As a result, internal struggles characterized the Albanian nobility throughout the fourteenth century. External
threats to the country stimulated a process of centralization
to provide for a common defense, but the struggle for power
inevitably brought the nobles into conflict with one another.
At the same time, Venetian, and later Ottoman, interference
encouraged these domestic disputes. The ever-increasing
cost of warfare compounded this situation. Albania suffered
the same fate as most of Europe during this time for, as British historian Rodney Hilton pointed out, "Campaigns
tended to be longer and more sustained; more and more soldiers of all ranks were being paid cash wages; and the
equipment, from horses to fortifications, was becoming
more expensive."[21]

Rising prices, more frequent conflicts, and advances in
the technology of warfare all added to this dilemma. To
meet these rising costs the nobility needed to do one of two
things — either to increase the size of their holdings and
thereby their revenue base or to extract additional revenues
from an already overburdened peasantry. Complicating the
situation further, agricultural productivity did not experi-

------

[21]Hilton, "A Crisis of Feudalism," p. 13.

ence a similar increase, in part because the surplus production was not reinvested in agriculture. Even so, the most productive land was already under cultivation, and, more significantly, the population was declining due largely to warfare and the plague. As agriculture was labor intensive and the population in decline, resources steadily dwindled. Thus, the nobility came into conflict with one another as they fought for control of the limited resources available. In addition, Venetian intervention worked to assure that none of the contending parties gain the upper hand in this struggle, thereby worsening the conflict among the native aristocracy and impeding the development of a native merchant class.

Opposition to Venice extended to part of the nobility, as well as to the peasants. This is evidenced not only by the peasant uprisings, but also by a considerable contraband trade in Albanian wheat. Undoubtedly, much of this illegal trade was carried on by nobles, in violation of their agreements with the Republic of St. Mark, seeking to raise additional revenues to finance their domestic struggles and build their power bases. The Venetians bought Albanian wheat at fixed prices, below the market value; due to the high demand for this commodity, a better price could often be obtained by selling it elsewhere. Some of this contraband trade may also have been carried on by free peasant communities who needed resources to defend themselves against attempts to encroach upon their traditional liberty; a situation in itself resulting from the struggle of the nobility to gain additional revenues. Venetian influence on the Albanian coast was so strong that, as a nineteenth century traveler observed, "Italian is understood by many of the Christian merchants here, being the language of commerce on these coasts."[22]

In a revealing analysis, Traian Stoianovich explained that the process of the native aristocracy allying themselves with foreign merchants was common throughout the region: "In the Balkans, a crucial aspect of this conflict [between lords and peasants] was the attempt on the part of the lords, patricians, or aristocrats to transform themselves into a largely closed estate, ally themselves with powerful foreign merchants, seize the land and revenues of the peasantry, and curb the aspirations of native 'middle elements,' regardless of whether these were a potentially rising group."[23]

The general crisis in Europe during the fourteenth and fifteenth centuries also manifested itself in Albania. The increasing influence of Venice and the Ottoman Empire worsened this crisis and led to rebellions and conflicts. Out of these conflicts arose George Castriota Scanderbeg and his famous struggle to oppose Islamic domination of his homeland, which, it must also be remembered, directed itself against Venetian Imperialism as well.

---

[22]Knight, *Albania*, p. 113.

[23]Stoianovich, *A Study in Balkan Civilization*, p. 130.

Chapter II
The Ottoman Threat to Albania

"Lo one, whom later age has brought to light,
Matchable to the greatest of the great:
Great both in name, and great in power and might,
And meriting a mere triumphant feat.

The scourge of Turks, and plague of Infidels,
Thy acts, o Scanderbeg, this volume tells."

— Edmund Spenser[24]

Ottoman influence in Albania grew rapidly as the fourteenth century drew to a close. The century of famine, climatic changes, and plague had also witnessed the entry of a new political and religious force in Europe when the Ottoman Turks crossed the Bosphorus, at the request of one of the rival Byzantine ruling families then engaged in a civil war, and established themselves on the continent in 1354. Ottoman power in the southeastern part of the continent grew rapidly. The Sultans first brought Bulgaria under their control, establishing their capital at Adrianople [Edirne].

---

[24]Preface to Z.I. Gentleman, *The Famous Acts of George Castrioti.*

Next, they gradually dismembered the remnants of the former Serbian Empire of Stephan Dušan.

The Islamic invasion of the Balkan peninsula did not directly affect Albania until 1385 when Charles Thopia, a noble in the central part of the country, appealed to Sultan Murad I for military assistance against his northern neighbor
the Balsha family; an invitation which the Ottoman ruler
gladly accepted. This exemplifies the usual method used by
the Sultans to extend their power. Alarmed by the Ottoman
threat, the Venetians encouraged the formation of an alliance of Albanian aristocrats to oppose Thopia and the Ottomans. This coalition, however, met defeat at the battle of
Vjosa River after which most of the Albanian nobles accepted the suzerainty of the Sultan. Perhaps some saw alliance with the Turks as a means to escape from Venetian
domination, certainly such an ideal led Thopia to call in the
Ottomans as he hoped to use foreign assistance to disrupt
the balance of power amongst the native nobility which the
agents of the Republic of St. Mark had been trying to per-
petuate.

Though it marked the entry of the Ottomans into Albania, the outcome of this conflict did not significantly alter
the status quo in the country. The allegiance of the Albanian
nobility to the Sultan did not last long after the departure of
the Ottoman forces and the Venetian economic monopoly
remained unbroken. The nobility, however, confronted an
even more desperate need for revenues now that the Otto-

man threat had materialized. Thus, the entry of the Ottomans into Albania aggravated the political, social, and economic crisis in the country.

As the Ottoman peril intensified, many Albanians joined the Balkan coalition which fought the Sultan's armies at the battle of Kosovo-Polje in 1389, a conflict waged on Albanian territory, though it is remembered as being the death blow to the Serbian nobility for the remnants of Dušan's Empire ruled there at the time of the conflict. It was after the disastrous defeat of the Balkan forces that the Ottomans established a more permanent presence in Albania. Sultan Bayezid I, who succeeded his father Murad I, killed at the battle of Kosovo, allowed the Albanian lords to retain their lands in exchange for accepting his suzerainty and paying an annual tribute; in other words, to respect the obligations which they had sworn to keep to his father four years earlier.

Still, Bayezid had no better success in coercing the Albanians to respect these obligations than his father had. Thus, in 1394, he undertook a campaign in the country to subdue his recalcitrant vassals, gaining control of the southern part of the country, where he introduced the *timar* system.[25] At this time, he also introduced the *devshirme*, the tax on children to raise soldiers for the janissary corps, in Albania. This proved possible in the southern part of the country

---

[25]Doukas, *Decline and Fall of Byzantium*, pp. 87-88.

where the mountains did not provide the same natural defensive barrier as in the north, making it more susceptible to
Ottoman control. The *timar* system was used to displace nobles disloyal to the Sultan. The centralized Ottoman administration provided a certain stability to the region, as the
southern part of the country did not participate in the uprisings of the 1430s or in Scanderbeg's resistance.[26] It was
only later in 1480, as we shall see, that the southern part of
Albania joined the anti-Ottoman struggle.

Ottoman influence in Albania suffered a setback in 1402
when the Mongol leader Tamerlane, in an effort to recreate
the Empire of Ghenghis Khan, defeated the Turks at Ankara, and took Sultan Bayezid I prisoner. Bayezid died in
captivity the following year. This led to a struggle for the
throne on the part of his four sons, for the Ottomans had no
established rules for succession. Some Albanians partici-
pated in the battle at Ankara, and most sided with Bayezid's
son Musa in the ensuing civil war.[27]

This conflict ended in 1413 with the victory of another
of Bayezid's sons, Mehmed, who established his authority
over the Empire. With the collapse of the Mongol threat following the death of Tamerlane and the victory of Mehmed
I, the Ottoman Empire survived the most serious political
crisis of its early history. Nevertheless, it was a setback. During the interim Venice moved to strengthen its authority in

---

[26]Inalcik, "Timariotes chrétiens," p. 129.

[27]Doukas, *Decline and Fall of Byzantium*, p. 108.

northern and central Albania. The political chaos of the early years of the fifteenth century further worsened the political, social, and economic crisis in Albania. The trend towards centralization continued, despite Venetian efforts to halt it. As a result of these conflicts among the Albanian nobility, three large principalities dominated central and northern Albania: the Dukagjins in the north, the Castriotas in the north-central part of the country, and the Aranitis in the central part.

After establishing his control over the Empire, Sultan Mehmed I launched a campaign against Albania in 1415, reasserting Ottoman authority over the central and southern parts of the country. In the south, the *timar* system was extended, while in the central part of the country the aristocracy maintained their lands by paying tribute and sending their sons as hostages to the Ottoman court at Adrianople.[28]

Peasant unrest grew in the country as the nobility had to extract additional revenues from them [or find new sources of revenue, such as contraband trade of agricultural goods in violation of their accords with Venice or trying to bring additional territories under their control thus increasing conflicts between rival lords and adding a new financial burden] to meet the cost of Ottoman suzerainty. These new burdens, imposed as a direct result of the Turkish invasions,

---

[28]Inalcik, "Timariotes chrétiens," pp. 120, 122; and Doukas, *Decline and Fall of Byzantium*, pp. 115-116, who indicates that Albanians already served in high positions in the Ottoman Empire during the reign of Mehmed I.

explain, in part, the growing anti-Ottoman feeling among the peasantry.

The situation in the south, where the *timar* system was already in place, was different because the native aristocracy had been displaced or incorporated into the centrally controlled Ottoman system which strictly regulated the amount of revenues to be paid by each village on the basis of a land survey, or Cadaster. Each village was carefully surveyed, recording the male population and capital, and the tax burden distributed according to the ability of the community to pay. This system, in the beginning, actually decreased the overall financial burden imposed on the peasants, bringing a certain order and stability to the region.

Chapter III
Prelude to Rebellion

"Events are the master,
man alone has nothing in his hands."

— Oruç, "Tevârih-i âl-i osman-it"[29]

The Castriotas were an Albanian family from the village of Kastrat in the district of Has, a mountainous region of northeastern Albania. They were not a family of long-standing aristocratic origins. As the Albanian noble John Muzaka, a contemporary of Scanderbeg, later recalled in his memoirs, "the grandfather of the Lord Scanderbeg, the Lord Pal Castriota, did not have more than two villages named Sinja and Lower Gardi."[30] Pal Castriota may have been a village chieftain in Kastrat and made money by engaging in trade, using this revenue to move to the Dibra area and purchase these villages.

---

[29]Oruç, "Tevârih-i âl-i osman-it" in *Lufta shqiptaro-turke ne shekullin XV*, p. 45 (f. 53).

[30]"Gjon Muzaka mbi Kastriotet," doc, 150 in *Burime te zgjedhura për historine e Shqiperise*, vol. II, p. 232.

In any event, Pal's son John, who began his activities about 1390, expanded the family holdings to include the region between the upper Mati and lower Drin rivers. Like other Albanian nobles, John Castriota became an Ottoman vassal following the campaign of Bayezid I in 1394. With the temporary collapse of the Empire, he further extended his lands, at times allying himself with the Venetians. This expansionary policy was motivated by the causes we have already discussed — security and the need for additional revenues. He succeeded in extending his lands to include a large portion of north-central Albania, stretching from the upper Mati River in the north, to Tirana in the south, and from the Adriatic Sea to Dibra in the east.

As he now controlled one of the most economically prosperous regions of the country, John Castriota soon became one of the leading Albanian noblemen. The Mati River gave him access to the Adriatic Sea and allowed him to exploit the agricultural and timber resources of his lands and free himself from the Venetian economic monopoly. John Castriota's independence is attested to by the trade agreement he concluded with Venice's chief rival in the Adriatic, the Republic of Ragusa, in 1420, permitting their merchants to trade freely in his lands, which stretched from the coast all the way to Prizren.[31] This economic freedom increased the power and prestige of Scanderbeg's father. As early as

---

[31]"Marreveshje tregtare midis Gjon Kastriotit dhe Republikes se Raguzes, 25 shkurt 1420," doc. 152 in *Burime te zgjedhura*, vol. II, p. 233.

1413, both Venice and Ragusa recognized the political and economic importance of his lands when they made John Castriota an honorary citizen.[32]

John Castriota enhanced his power and territory through a combination of political savvy and military prowess, characteristics his son would also demonstrate. He increased his holdings not only through conflicts with neighboring nobles, but also through marriage. "From this Pal was born the Lord John Castriota, who was made the ruler of Mati, and from him was born the Lord Scanderbeg," John Muzaka recalled, "And the mother of the Lord Scanderbeg, the wife of Lord John, had the name Voisova Tribalda and came from a good family."[33] He also married his daughters into neighboring aristocratic families, one of them becoming the wife of Stephan Crnojevič, the ruler of Zeta [Montenegro].[34]

Religion was another political instrument employed by John Castriota. After the Ottoman invasion in 1415, when he again became a vassal of the Sultan, he adopted Islam; but, he regularly changed religions according to the political situation in which he found himself, as the Albanian Bishop Fan S. Noli observed, becoming Catholic when allied with

---

[32]Ducellier, "Principauté des Kastriote," p. 136.

[33]"Gjon Muzaka mbi Kastriotet," doc. 150 in *Burime te zgjedhura*, vol. II, p. 232.

[34] Skendi, "Complex Environment of Skenderbeg's Activity," p. 169.

Map of Fifteenth Century Albania

the Venetians, Orthodox when allied with Serbia, and Moslem when he accepted the suzerainty of the Sultan.[35]

John Castriota had nine children, four sons and five daughters. His youngest son, George, was born around 1405. After Mehmed I's campaign in 1415, John Castriota, like other Albanian nobles, sent his sons to Adrianople as hostages. The Albanian nobleman John Muzaka recorded that "He [George] had been given by him [John Castriota] to the aforementioned Murad... He was called George Castriota, but when he was made a Turk, he was called Scanderbeg, because Skender means Alexander and beg means lord."[36] They remained there until 1420, when all of them were again in Albania. In 1423, Sultan Murad II launched a new invasion in the country to subdue recalcitrant nobles. John Castriota again pledged loyalty to the Sultan and this time sent three of his sons, including George, to the Ottoman capital. In 1426, his sons are again found in Albania, but after this date the whereabouts of his youngest son George are unknown.

During his stay in Adrianople, George Castriota was educated at the Palace School and instructed in the military arts; he later converted to Islam and took the name *Scander* [*Iskendër*, meaning Alexander]. He may have served with

---

[35]Noli, *George Castrioti Scanderbeg*, p. 21.

[36]"Nga Gjenealogjia e bujarit shqiptar Gjon Muzaka," doc. 177 in *Burime te zgjedhura*, vol. II, p. 278.

Ottoman armies on campaigns in Anatolia during his second stay at Adrianople. After 1426, he served in various
capacities, at different times, in the Ottoman Army. At some
point, he earned the title of beg, implying the rank of general, and thus he became known as Scanderbeg.

In 1428, war broke out between Venice and the Ottomans over the port city of Salonika on the Aegean coast.
Hoping to escape from Ottoman control, John Castriota and
other Albanian leaders allied themselves with the Venetians. The Ottoman chronicler Oruç recorded: "[Sultan Mu-
rad] gathered heavily armed soldiers and attacked the fortress of Salonika, saying that this was a holy war. They made
a great war and with the help of cannons destroyed the
city's walls, yet the Infidels were not subdued. The Padishah, in the name of God, ordered that they begin to pillage.
The fortress was then taken." When they suffered defeat in
1430, the Venetians abandoned their Albanian allies, leaving them to face the wrath of Sultan Murad II who launched
a new invasion in the country. Oruç continued: "the lands
of John Castriota were also taken, and many other fortresses
were conquered."[37] This campaign ended with many Albanian nobles being displaced. John Castriota lost large portions of his principality to the Ottomans, but retained the
largely mountainous portion of his former lands by again
swearing allegiance to the Sultan.

---

[37]Oruç, "Tevarih-i al-i osman-it," Burime osmane, p. 43 [f. 114]

The disloyalty of the Albanian nobility during the war with Venice led the Porte to extend the *timar* system to include most of central Albania. During 1431 and 1432, Ottoman officials conducted a land and population survey in the region and established 335 *timars*; while many of the Albanian nobles were displaced, some powerful lords such as John Castriota and George Araniti had sufficient power to retain portions of their former lands. Still others preserved their social status by allying themselves with the Ottomans and becoming *timar* holders. Many of these converted to Islam, although a considerable portion did not do so. Of the 335 *timars*, approximately half were granted to Albanians, a third of whom were Christians; the rest being given to Turks from Anatolia. [38]

The Ottoman efforts to extend the *timar* system into the central part of the country met with strong resistance. Many nobles fought to retain their lands. Meanwhile, the peasants opposed the extension of Ottoman control because of the *devshirme*, which led to the conscription of their most able-bodied children into military service, depriving the village community of valuable labor and violating local tradition. The peasants also blamed the Ottomans for the increasing fiscal burden they had borne since the beginning of the century. Free peasants in the mountainous regions actively op-

---

[38]On this land survey, see Inalcik, "Timariotes chrétiens," pp. 125, 130, and 138; Fine, *Late Medieval Balkans*, p. 535; and Nicol, *The Despotate of Epiros*, p. 204.

posed efforts to incorporate their villages into the *timar* system as they struggled to maintain their independence. A contemporary of these events, the chronicler Kritoboulos, testifies: "[The Albanians were] determined to be autonomous and free in every way, and were unwilling to pay a yearly tax, as did all their neighbors, or to furnish troops for expeditions, either to the Sultan's father [Murad II] or to the Sultan himself [Mehmed II], or to obey him at all."[39]

The question poses itself as to why the Ottomans were able to impose the *timar* system in the southern part of the country without great opposition, while in the central regions they encountered fierce resistance. The answer is to be found in the existence of numerous free peasant communities, the greater geographic isolation of the area, and that nearly forty years of hostilities between the Albanians and the Turks had created many bitter feelings.

The expansion of Ottoman control led to widespread revolts in central Albania as Turkish spahis came to claim their *timars*. Andrew Thopia, a noble displaced by Murad II's invasion, led the first major revolt which defeated a small Turkish detachment. The Ottoman chronicler Oruç records for the year 836 (1432-33) that "Ali bey, the son of Evrenos bey, attacked the vilayet of the Albanians. It did not go favorably for him. Ali bey was defeated."[40]

---

[39]Kritovoulos, *History of Mehmed the Conqueror*, pp. 210-211 [V, 61]

[40]Oruç, "Tevarih-i al-i osman-it," in *Burime Osmane*, p. 44 (f. 115).

Thopia's success led others, such as John Castriota and George Araniti, to renounce their allegiance to the Sultan and to try to regain their lost territories. Between 1433 and 1436 Albanian rebellions defeated three separate Ottoman armies sent by Murad II to quell the uprisings. Finally, in 1436, the Sultan sent a large army, again led by Ali Bey, that crushed most of the uprisings; "[They] pillaged and destroyed the lands of John Castriota, the men were put to the sword, while the women were made slaves," Oruç records, "They completely conquered Janina and Kanina and returned with great plunder... The son of Evrenos bey conquered the vilayet of the Albanians and was satiated with plunder from pillaging."[41] Only George Araniti managed to maintain a small pocket of resistance in the mountains of central Albania. Widespread opposition to the Ottomans remained, leading to a new revolt in Berat in 1437, but this new uprising was quickly suppressed by the Sultan's forces.

These rebellions were doomed to failure as they lacked any central organization or leadership, but rather were separate local events; lacking any coordination of manpower and resources, the well-trained, highly organized, and disciplined Ottoman troops had a distinct advantage over the Albanians. While both nobles and peasants united in their opposition to the Ottomans, at this stage it failed to bring about any form of political or military unity. Despite their

---

[41]Oruç, "Tevarih-i al-i osman-it," in *Burime Osmane*, p. 44 (f. 115).

George Castriota Scanderbeg

failure, the rebellions of the 1430s laid important founda-
tions for the revolt led by Scanderbeg later on. The Albanians gradually learned that they needed to mobilize vast resources and create a unified opposition to resist successfully
the power of the Sultan's armies.

After his defeat by the Ottomans in 1436, John Castriota
lost possession of most of his lands. He died shortly there-
after, a broken man. George Castriota is again found in Albania in 1437, serving as a spahi in the Dibra region. He had
played no part in the uprisings of the previous years, having
served loyally with the Ottoman army in Anatolia. Undoubtedly, Scanderbeg's status as a hostage played a part in
his father's political strategy. John Castriota wanted to make
certain that he had some leverage with each of the main foreign powers in Albania; while George served with the Sultan's forces, his older brother, Stanish, served with the Venetians. Certainly, Scanderbeg remained loyal to his father
who preferred that his son serve the Sultan, despite his own
battle to free his lands from Ottoman influence. John Castriota was a pragmatic politician and realized, especially after
the recovery of the Ottoman Empire following its devastating defeat by Tamerlane and the ensuing civil war, that the
Ottoman threat would not disappear. Thus, to have a son
serve in the Ottoman army helped to preserve the family's
influence with this powerful foe.

The success of this policy is evidenced by the fact that,
after John Castriota's death, Scanderbeg received a *timar* in

a portion of his father's former territory. The Serbian Janissary Konstantin Mihailović, another contemporary chronicler, is incorrect when he claims that Scanderbeg "asked that
he [Murad II] give him the land of Ivan [John Castriota], but
he did not tell him that he was Ivan's son."[42] Certainly, such
an important fact would not have escaped the attention of
the Porte when assigning *timars*. The Sultan may even have
been compelled to send Scanderbeg to Albania as a response
to political repercussions following the death of John Castriota. In any event, it must be seen as a reward for his loyal
service and an attempt to pacify the rebellious Albanians by
installing native officials in administrative positions whom
the Sultan believed could be trusted. According to Marin
Barletti, Scanderbeg himself is said to have proclaimed:
"Although we lived together as a family, as it were, in one
and the same course of life, although we ate at the same ta-
ble and though we did in a manner breathe jointly with one
and the same soul, nevertheless, neither they nor any man
alive ever heard me mention my country... Neither was
there any man that heard me use any speech, or utter any
word at any time, which might reveal me to be a Christian
or a free man."[43]

Determined to continue the policies of his father, he secretly dreamed of regaining possession of the family lands

---

[42]Mihailović, *Memoirs of a Janissary*, pp. 134-135.

[43]Translated in Nelo Drizari, *Scanderbeg: His Life, Correspondence, Orations, Victories, and Philosophy*, p. 2.

and freeing them from Ottoman domination. A shrewd politician, Scanderbeg had learned from the experiences of his father and the unsuccessful rebellions of the 1430s and realized that he had to be cautious and patient in pursuing his goals. His chance came, a contemporary chronicler records, when the Sultan received news that the Governor of Croya, the most important fortress in central Albania, which had formerly been part of John Castriota's lands, had died, and Scanderbeg, "being a capable man and a faithful servant of the said Lord [Murad II], took the duty of subashi of Croya, a duty he took on willingly and thus was sent to his land. He remained loyal for some years... endeavoring to win the friendship and goodwill of the people of that place and secretly he informed his majesty King Alphonso [V, of Naples], that his desire was to revolt against the Turk."[44]

During his tenure as Governor of Croya, Scanderbeg entered into secret negotiations with Venice and Ragusa, hoping to build a base of support for future political and military action. After a couple of years, Scanderbeg left Croya to become Governor of Dibra, another important fortress in the eastern part of his father's former territories, where he continued to conduct a secret foreign policy, remaining in contact with Naples and Hungary.

---

[44]"Nga vepra e historianit italian Donado de Lece," dok. 186 in *Burime te zgjedhura*, vol. II, p. 281.

George Castriota Scanderbeg

Chapter IV
The Revolt of 1443 and the Organization of the Albanian Resistance to Islamic Domination Led by Scanderbeg

"Anon from the castle walls
The crescent banner falls,
And the crowd beholds instead,
Like a portent in the sky,
Iskander's banner fly,
The Black Eagle with double head
And a shout ascends on high,
For men's souls are tired of the Turks,
And their wicked ways and works,
That have made of Ak-hissar
A city of the plague;
And the loud exultant cry
That echoes wide and far
Is `Long Live Scanderbeg!'"

— Henry Wadsworth Longfellow[45]

While serving as Governor of Dibra, in 1443, Scanderbeg accompanied the Ottoman army on campaign against

---

[45]Henry Wadsworth Longfellow, "The Spanish Jew's Second Tale: Scanderbeg," in *The Complete Writings of Henry Wadsworth Longfellow*, vol. IV,
p. 266.

the Christian forces led by John Hunyadi, the Governor of Hungary, who had launched an offensive into Serbia to restore George Branković to the throne of that principality. The two armies met at Niš, on 3 November 1443, where the Ottomans met with a decisive defeat by the Christian forces and began a hasty retreat. Hunyadi's forces were not prepared, however, to continue the offensive and, having achieved their immediate objective, withdrew. Realizing the opportunity that this conflict presented, Scanderbeg carefully prepared his strategy in advance. Amidst the chaotic retreat of the Islamic forces, he abandoned the Ottoman army, together with 300 loyal Albanian soldiers who had accompanied him to Niš; they seized the Imperial Secretary and forced him to issue a *firman* [imperial decree] naming him Governor of Croya before killing him so as to keep their intentions secret.

The Albanian nobleman John Muzaka recounted the events this way: "When the Turk sent the Pasha of Rumelia against the Hungarians, he also sent Scanderbeg with him; there the aforementioned Pasha was beaten and the Turks fled; Scanderbeg escaped with the others. By chance the secretary of the Pasha was found with him; Scanderbeg seized him and forced him to issue, in the name of the Sultan, an order for the Governor of Croya to surrender the fortress and its lands to him. Although he objected, the secretary fulfilled his wishes; then, Scanderbeg killed him so that he not reveal what had been done. Then Scanderbeg, with the several hundred Albanians who were with him, set off and, as soon as he arrived in Albania and entered Croya, he gave the order to the Governor, who then surrendered the fortress to him; thus he [Scanderbeg] became lord of Croya, a powerful land. Because of this all the nobles of Albania were very glad and Scanderbeg became a Christian again."[46]

Imperial decree in hand, Scanderbeg returned to Albania with single-minded purpose. Upon reaching Dibra, he organized the local population in support of his rebellion and began his march to Croya. The mountain fortress of Croya was the key to central Albania and to reclaiming his father's lands; it was also the richest part of the country with the greatest potential to provide the resources necessary to resist the Ottomans. The ensuing chaos in the aftermath of the Ottoman defeat at Niš allowed Scanderbeg time to execute his plan in secrecy. There was no one to warn the Ottoman garrisons of the impending revolt; on 27 November, the rebels neared the walls of Croya. Scanderbeg sent his nephew Hamsa into the city with the *firman* instructing the Ottoman Governor Hasan Beg to turn over command of the fortress to Scanderbeg. Having no reason to suspect that the order was false, the Governor complied and turned over command of the citadel to Scanderbeg; he then left for Adrianople to await reassignment. While the bulk of Scanderbeg's men remained outside the city, so as not to arouse suspicion, they secretly entered in the middle of the night, like

---

[46]"Bujari Gj. Muzaka mbi kthimin e Skenderbeut ne Krujë," dok. 189 in *Burime te zgjedhura*, vol. II, pp. 285-286.

the Greeks before Troy, and the Albanians carried out their plan, killing most of the Ottoman garrison.[47]

The next day, in the city's cathedral, Scanderbeg proclaimed his independence from the Ottomans and told his followers: "It is not I who has given you this nation and superiority. It is not I who has given you this city. It is you who have given them unto me. It was not I who put arms into your hands. I found you ready in arms. I found you everywhere bearing the signs of liberty in your hearts, in your faces, in your swords, and in your lances. And, as most loyal teachers and guardians ordained by my father, you have put the scepter in my hands with no less faith and diligence than as if you had kept and preserved it especially for me even until this day. And you have brought me by your effort and careful care into my ancestral possession without shedding any blood. Now, therefore, in the name of God, lead on and conduct me into the recovery of the rest of our country, which yet remains in the hands and possession of the enemy. The greatest part and, in a manner, the whole task you have accomplished: Croya is recovered. And this territory therefore is wholly under our care. The Dibrans and all the people are now united with us. The name of the enemy banished from this part of our country. Only the towns and strongholds are still in enemy hands.... Let us then march on and advance our standards speedily. Let us take unto us the

---

[47]Moore, *George Castriot*, p. 26; Knolles, *Generall Historie of the Turkes*, p. 284.

Scanderbeg entering Croya, November 27, 1443

courage of victors. Fortune shall favor our endeavors..."[48] He then renounced Islam in favor of Catholicism and decreed that all Muslims in the city follow his example and immediately convert or be executed.

This was not a sudden flash of religious fervor or some sort of divine revelation. Scanderbeg had been a Muslim in name only; like his father, who changed faiths according to his political alliances, he too used religion to achieve his political goals. As the Ottomans were the principal threat to his lands, he outlawed Islam as a symbolic act of defiance against the Sultan, the spiritual leader of the Islamic faith. It also had a practical significance, for as Islam had been adopted by Albanians for purely political purposes, a Muslim, therefore, by definition, was an ally of the Sultan and thus an enemy of the rebellion. Indeed, according to Barletti, few accepted this offer: "The greater part of the Turks chose to encounter the threatened destruction rather than abjure their religion, and fell by the hands of the Christians, or by their own act... Those who consented to be baptized were well provided for at the public charge. A strict watch, however, was kept upon them, until such time as they should appear to be well settled into their new faith."[49]

In addition to these domestic considerations, Scanderbeg realized the need for foreign support to resist Ottoman

---

[48] According to Barletti, translated in Drizari, *Scanderbeg*, pp. 3-4.

[49] Moore, *George Castriot*, p. 27.

domination; this meant appealing to the Pope and the Catholic states of Europe, with whom he had been in contact since he first returned to Albania as part of the Ottoman administration, for financial and material assistance. The Albanians certainly expected a crusade against the Turkish Infidels to be undertaken, especially after the victory at Niš. Upon proclaiming his independence from Ottoman domination, Scanderbeg raised the red banner of the Castriota family, with a double-headed black eagle in the center, over the fortress of Croya. This banner remained a defiant symbol of independence, eventually becoming the national flag of Albania.

As news of the Ottoman defeat at Niš spread throughout the mountains of Albania, fueled by Scanderbeg's revolt, successful uprisings against the Turks broke out spontaneously. "In the general destruction of the Turks," Barletti informs us, "the governor of Croya, while on his way to Adrianople, was also attacked and slain, together with all his retinue, and his baggage seized and plundered."[50]

George Araniti, who had continued a small-scale guerilla war since his defeat by the Ottomans in 1436, joined the revolt, reclaiming his former lands. Like Araniti, Scanderbeg received mass support and with a hastily gathered army marched on the remaining Ottoman fortresses in central Albania, reclaiming the Castriota lands. Meanwhile, Sfiet-

---

[50]Moore, *George Castriot*, p. 28.

grade, on the eastern border of the Albanian lands, was garrisoned and fortified, both to cut off the retreat of the Turks still trapped in the country and to be an outpost to resist future invasions from this direction. The chaos following the defeat at Niš and the approaching winter prohibited Ottoman reinforcements from aiding Turkish garrisons in Albania, so they quickly surrendered to the rebels.

The ease of these early victories surprised even Scanderbeg who proclaimed: "We must thank God for causing our enemies to deliver into our hands and possession of so goodly and strong fortresses without any slaughter or bloodshed."[51] By the end of 1443 northern and central Albania had been completely freed from Ottoman occupation.

The experience of the 1430s had proven to the Albanian nobility that some form of unity was essential to resist the Ottoman advance successfully. A lack of political unity had been the principal cause for failure in previous Albanian encounters with the Sultan's armies. Konstantin Mihailović, a veteran of the janissary corps, noted: "The reason he [the Sultan] defeated them [the Albanians] so easily was that one looked on while he was defeating another."[52] With this problem in mind, Scanderbeg and other Albanian nobles met at Alessio [Lezhë, in Albanian], a port city controlled by Venice on the Adriatic coast. The meeting took place at the

---

[51]According to Barletti, translated in Drizari, *Scanderbeg*, p. 6.

[52]Mihailović, *Memoirs of a Janissary*, p. 135.

cathedral of St. Nicholas on 2 March 1444. Venetian representatives attended the meeting as observers, interested in protecting their coastal possessions from Ottoman aggression, as well as hoping to prevent any Albanian leader from becoming so powerful that they could threaten Venetian territories or break their economic monopoly. Despite some hesitation by those who preferred to wait for the organization of a Christian crusade, the Albanian nobility agreed to pool their resources and organize a unified military resistance to the Ottomans.

His military and administrative experience, combined with his first-hand knowledge of the Ottomans made Scanderbeg the logical choice as General of the new army. Barletti recalled: "He was unanimously chosen the commander-in-chief of the armies, and to his sole direction was committed the conduct of the war. He was esteemed most worthy of the honor bestowed upon him on account of his skill and science in military affairs, his great prudence and deliberation, his long acquaintance with the manners and customs of the barbarians, and his wonderful judgement, which was confirmed by long use and daily experience."[53] Added to these considerations, he also controlled the wealthiest part of Albania and his lands were centrally located, including the key fortress of Croya.

At Alessio, Castriota implored the other Albanian leaders: "Do not delay and tarry so long, till you see some aid

---

[53]Moore, *George Castriot*, p. 44.

The League of Alession, March 2, 1444

coming. Then it will be too late to implore your supporters. But even now rather, and presently joining your forces with our forces and your arms with our arms, let us drive and compel the enemy speedily to take the field, or let us be the first upon him and invade his territories."[54]

A contemporary of these events, John Muzaka, recorded: "Then these rulers of Albania were gathered in an assembly at Alessio. Some went themselves, while others sent their lieutenants, and the aforementioned Scanderbeg was made chief leader of Albania, and each of them [the nobles] sent men and money according to the amount that belonged to him. Several sons of these nobles also fought under his direction, both to learn the art of war, as well as to defend their estates. Being a powerful lord and strong in war and brave, he was chosen leader by all of them and they followed him."[55]

The authority granted to Scanderbeg as General of the Army was strictly limited; each of the nobles preserved his autonomy in his own domains. He was seen as first among equals. The League of Alessio, as it came to be called, was a weak organization; each of the nobles jealously guarding their privileges and attempting to do only the minimum necessary to form an effective resistance to the Turks. The distrust built up over years of conflict among themselves

---

[54]According to Barletti, translated in Drizari, *Scanderbeg*, p. 12.

[55]"Bujari Gj. Muzaka mbi Kuvendin e Lezhës," Dok. 191 in *Burime të zgjedhura*, vol. II, p. 289.

had not disappeared. Scanderbeg, on the other hand, knowing quite well the strengths and weaknesses of his enemy, realized the need for a strong centralized organization capable of mobilizing the resources necessary to maintain the independence of the Albanian lands. In his book, *The Papacy and the Levant*, the American historian Kenneth Setton recognized the difference between the two visions: the nobles, "looked back with nostalgia upon a chaotic past, and Scanderbeg looked forward to the establishment of a centralized Christian state."[56]

For the time being, the League of Alessio served as a vehicle for Scanderbeg to achieve his goals. He realized that the key to success against the powerful Ottoman forces lay in organizing the mass of rebellious peasants and the rich resources of the country. To do this he traveled from village to village, throughout central Albania, to organize his defenses. His style and manners appealed to the peasantry; he dressed in plain clothes and ate the same food as his soldiers. This won the undying loyalty of his troops. Renowned historian Edward Gibbon tells us that, "the Albanians, a martial race, were unanimous to live and die with their hereditary prince."[57]

While the lessons of previous decades had taught Albanian leaders that some form of centralized organization was

---

[56]Setton, *The Papacy and the Levant*, vol. II, p. 195.

[57]Gibbon, *Decline and Fall of the Roman Empire*, vol. III, p. 742.

necessary to oppose Ottoman might, the opportunities offered by serving with Scanderbeg also must have appealed
to many peasants. They could expect ranks and rewards
commensurate with their abilities, he told them: "I will
judge your merits when I see your swords smoking with the
blood of the Turks: when I myself both as an observer and
encourager will imitate your prowess, being prodigal both
of life and safety. At that time, I will heap upon you all sorts
of commendations and rewards..." The Albanian leader
continued: "But he who should stand in fear of the lieutenants of Murad... certainly in my opinion would be unworthy
both of the name and the sword he bears, and unworthy of
the air which makes him breathe and live."[58]

Clearly, Scanderbeg did not seek to alter the fundamen-
tal social structure of the land; rather he sought to bring
about an end to the feudal anarchy which had plagued the
country and to remove the foreign influences which had encouraged it. Indeed, this implied a greater social mobility
that naturally attracted the loyalty of the peasants who
formed the bulk of his army. No one – neither Scanderbeg,
the other nobles, nor the peasants – had any awareness of
changing the social or economic structure. The peasants
sought to preserve their traditional liberties within the
framework of the feudal-tribal society; the nobles feared the

---

[58] According to Barletti, translated in Drizhari, *Scanderbeg*, pp. 16-17; see
also *George Kastriot-Scanderbeg and the Albanian-Turkish War*, p. 78.

loss of their individual political and social status. Scander-beg's objective was not to overthrow feudalism, but to create a professional, standing army, with organized and prepared reserve forces, in the context of a centralized feudal-tribal state commensurate with the social and economic conditions existing in the Albanian lands in the fifteenth century.

He recruited soldiers unquestionably loyal to him on the basis of one man from each household. This was done to spread out the burden of defense so that no village bore an unequal share and so as not to diminish significantly the manpower necessary to care for the flocks and cultivate the fields because the economic strength of the country would be critical in providing the resources necessary to defend Albania against the Ottomans. By May, 1444, Scanderbeg had organized a standing army of 8,000 troops, supplemented by a reserve force of 7,000 to 10,000 men which could be rapidly mobilized in times of crisis. "It was a matter of great wonder," Venetian chronicler Marin Barletti noted, "to both the friends and foes of Scanderbeg, that he should take the field with so few forces, when he might have had so much larger an army under his command. But Scanderbeg himself was wont to say, that the quality of an army was more to be depended upon than the size of it."[59] He also

---

[59]Moore, *George Castriot*, p. 46.

organized an intelligence service which could quickly transmit information about Ottoman activities from village to village throughout the land.[60]

The revolt begun in 1443 united Albanians as they realized the necessity of military cooperation in face of the Islamic peril, but clearly the political and economic unity which this demanded threatened many who stood to lose their privileges to the centralized feudal state envisioned by Scanderbeg.

Cavalry, using a small, fleet breed of horses raised in the mountains of Albania, formed the main body of Scanderbeg's regular army. The horsemen were lightly armed, usually with swords, spears, lances, or bows and arrows. As peasants composed the majority of the army, Scanderbeg needed to raise revenues to properly equip and to pay his soldiers who received a salary of between three and five ducats per month,[61] as well as to strengthen the fortresses in the country to withstand superior Ottoman firepower. The necessary revenues came from several sources: the funds contributed by the members of the League of Alessio, the revenues obtained from the sale of goods from the Castriota

---

[60]Moore, *George Castriot*, p. 136; Pollo and Puto, *History of Albania*, p. 73; *George Kastriot-Scanderbeg and the Albanian-Turkish War*, p. 57; and Frashëri, *Scanderbeg*, p. 19.

[61]Naci, "A propos de quelques truchements concernant les rapports de la Papauté avec Scanderbeg," p. 81.

lands in the north-central part of the country on the international market, and financial assistance received from the Pope and foreign governments.

Plunder taken during the raids into Ottoman territory also formed an important source of revenue; Scanderbeg is said to have proclaimed to his soldiers: "Behold here near at hand the territory of the enemy, rich and plentiful in wealth of all sorts. Your gallantry and prowess have made it naked and bare of all defense. Now, therefore, with good leisure and ease, charge and load yourselves with the prey and spoils, which are left and abandon to your pleasure and discretion."[62]

The spoils of war also played an important role in equipping his peasant army. After defeating one of the earliest Ottoman attempts to suppress the rebellion, the chronicler Barletti reported that Scanderbeg told his soldiers: "I do hereby order and appoint that the infantry shall take the horses of the slain enemies and that all of you from now on shall serve on horseback as Men at Arms."[63] This passage also reflects the prestige of the cavalry as a symbol of social status, and an indication of the leading role of mounted soldiers in the defense of the country.

As he organized his army, Scanderbeg personally inspected the citadels throughout the country and ordered repairs to be commenced immediately in preparation for an

---

[62]According to Barletti, translated in Drizari, *Scanderbeg*, pp. 18-19.

[63]According to Barletti, translated in Drizari, *Scanderbeg*, p. 19.

Ottoman invasion. They not only protected the land against invasion, but also guarded the reserves of food and weapons stored in mountain hideouts.[64]

Cannons, first used in the Balkans in the second half of the fourteenth century, also played a role in defending Albanian strongholds. While the Albanians may have produced some of their own firearms, as well as gunpowder (by mixing crushed sulphur, charcoal and saltpeter), the Republic of Ragusa, modern Dubrovnik, served as the principal supplier of these items in the region.[65] Djurdjica Petrović explains that "the Balkan princes and feudal lords, whose lands were increasingly threatened by the ever-deeper penetration of the Ottomans, turned to Dubrovnik for aid, seeking to borrow or buy firearms or gunpowder. As a result, Dubrovnik, in the course of the fifteenth century, increased its production of firearms to such a degree that it became the main supplier of these weapons to the Central Balkans."[66]

Although there is not enough evidence to determine the effectiveness of firearms in defending Albanian strongholds against the Turkish attacks, their role seems to have been limited judging from the fact that most fortresses conquered

---

[64]Isaku, "L'art militaire de Skanderbeg," pp. 172, 176; and Frashëri, *Scanderbeg*, p. 19.

[65]Isaku, "L'art militaire de Skanderbeg," p. 176; Drishti, "L'utilisation des armes à feu par les troupes de Skanderbeg," pp. 179-180.

[66]Petrović, "Firearms in the Balkans, " p. 180.

by either the Ottomans or by the Albanians were taken by trickery, siege, or other means, instead of as a direct result of bombardment. Clearly, the system of defensive fortresses and the highly mobile, lightly armed cavalry served as the most effective weapons to fend off the invaders in the mountains of Albania.

By organizing his army on a popular basis, with soldiers directly loyal to and dependent upon him, Scanderbeg defended himself against dissension in the ranks of the nobility, which he realized would resist his centralizing efforts. He also enhanced the loyalty of his troops by not setting himself apart from the common soldiers, sharing the same meals and sleeping quarters with his men. Drawing his information largely from Barletti, Edward Gibbon wrote of the Albanian leader that, "His manners were popular; but his discipline was severe; and every superfluous vice was banished from his camp."[67]

Scanderbeg's military experience with the Turks proved to be of great importance as he had a number of spies in the Ottoman armies who kept him informed of their movements. He stationed 3,000 troops on the eastern frontier of Albania to protect the mountain passes against an Ottoman invasion, under the command of Moisi Golemi, a noble loyal to Scanderbeg and one of his ablest commanders.

The powerful army Scanderbeg created shortly after his selection as General of the Army by the League of Alessio

---

[67]Gibbon, *Decline and Fall of the Roman Empire*, vol. III, p. 742.

Scanderbeg's lieutenant Moisi Golemi

made many of its members feel insecure. This led some of them to appeal to the Ottomans and/or the Venetians for assistance. Scanderbeg used his military power to strip these disloyal lords of their lands and he appointed loyal officers to administer these territories. The new lands were joined to the Castriota domains and administered by an appointed official. Traitorous nobles also lost their ranks and were replaced by soldiers of proven skill, regardless of their social origin.[68] The rebellion gradually changed its character as Scanderbeg moved to enhance his personal authority in violation of the agreement formed by the nobles at Alessio in 1444, who had envisioned it as an alliance of equals against a common foe.

While the Albanians organized a united defense under the leadership of Scanderbeg, the Ottomans remained occupied by the war with the Christian coalition led by the Kingdom of Hungary. The peace that ended the war in June, 1444, allowed the Ottomans to concentrate on putting down the rebellions that had broken out not only in Albania, but also in Greece, Anatolia, and elsewhere in the Empire. That same month an Ottoman army of 25,000 men, commanded by Ali Pasha, invaded Albania near Dibra. Scanderbeg, having received advanced warning of the Ottoman campaign from his spies, retreated before the enemy, leading them into the narrow valley of Torviolli where the Albanian

---

[68]Setton, *Papacy and the Levant,* vol II, p. 195; and Tradhëtia feudale sipas bujarit Gjon Muzaka, dok. 208 in *Burime të zgjedhura,* vol. II, p. 135.

forces waited to ambush the invaders. They surprised the Ottomans, attacking them on all sides, destroying the invading army, with very few Turkish soldiers able to escape.[69]

The element of surprise, combined with Scanderbeg's skillful use of the terrain in determining the location of the battle, allowed the Albanians to defeat the much larger Ottoman force. Additionally, the swift, lightly armed Albanian cavalry had a distinct advantage over the slower, heavily armed Ottoman spahis.

The Albanian victory drew the attention of the Pope and the governor of Transylvania and Hungary, John Hunyadi, who began to see Scanderbeg as an important element in a united Christian effort against the Turks.[70] Despite erroneous claims by several historians,[71] Scanderbeg did not participate in the Varna Crusade in the fall of 1444. His interest lay in defending his own territories. To venture across the Balkans, so far from his lands, would leave Albania vulnerable to attack; he could ill afford to take such a risk at a time when he was in the process of organizing his own defenses. Certainly, a decisive Christian victory would have relieved

---

[69]"Fitorja e parë e shqiptarëve kundër turqëve. Beteja e Torviollit," dok. 192 in *Burime të zgjedhura*, pp. 289-291; Moore, *George Castriot*, p. 46; and Knolles, *Generall Historie of the Turkes*, pp. 287-288.

[70]Docs. 9-10 in Radonić, *Gjuragj Kastrioti Skenderbeg*, pp. 5-7. See also Stavrou, *Etudes sur l'Albanie*, p. 75.

[71]For example, see Held, *Hunyadi: Legend and Reality*, p. 108; and Sugar, *A History of East Central Europe, Volume V: Southeastern Europe under Ottoman Rule, 1354-1801*, p. 29.

the pressure on Albania, but Scanderbeg realized that such an outcome was highly questionable.

Following the Ottoman victory at Varna, Murad II abdicated the throne and retired to Anatolia. His young son, Mehmed II, was unable to gain control of the Empire and faced opposition from the janissaries in the capital city of Adrianople who supported Osman Çelebi, a claimant to the throne. Scanderbeg took advantage of the political strife that ensued after Murad's retirement by increasing his raids on nearby Ottoman territories. These raids became so frequent that it was said that, "the possessions of the Sultan were the revenues of Scanderbeg."[72] Although the Porte tried to put an end to his rebellion, Ottoman invasions of Albania in 1445 and 1446 met with the same fate as that of Ali Pasha. The situation stabilized when Murad II reclaimed the throne in 1446 and soon after brought most of the Greek mainland back under Ottoman control, but Albania remained a thorn in the side of the Turkish Sultan.

Failing to subdue the Albanian rebels by force, Murad II next resorted to diplomatic initiatives, offering Scanderbeg a peace proposal: "Croya and your Father's Kingdom, although you have gained them by foul treachery, I give unto you, upon condition that you willingly restore unto me the other towns of Albania, which by no right belong to you but are mine by the Law of Arms, by myself honorably won. Whatever you have taken from my Father-in-law, the Prince

---

[72]Armstrong, *Heroes of Defeat*, p. 215.

of Serbia, you shall restore and make him an honorable rec-
ompense for the other harms you have done unto him. And
forever hereafter you shall as well refrain from doing vio-
lence to our friends or aid our enemies. Thus, shall you
avoid the displeasure of the Turks, but stand in my good
grace and favor as you have done before..."[73]

The Albanian leader rejected the Sultan's proposals outright: "I have not set down myself to contend with you in
foul and unbecoming language, but with Arms and the just
Fury of War."[74]

Scanderbeg's victories over the Ottomans increased his
power. The army gained confidence in its ability and this,
combined with the material rewards resulting from the Albanian successes, strengthened the loyalty of the troops toward their commander. This allowed Scanderbeg to increase his power base by seizing lands of neighboring nobles whom he distrusted and incorporating them into his
own domains. Scanderbeg, however, was unable to encroach upon the lands of the two most powerful noble families – the Dukagjins in the north of the country, and the Aranitis in the south-central part of Albania – whom he had to
continue to treat as allies.[75]

---

[73] According to Barletti, translated in Drizari, *Scanderbeg*, p. 27.

[74] According to Barletti, translated in Drizari, *Scanderbeg*, p. 28.

[75] Shuteriqi, "Les relations entre Skanderbeg et Georges Aranite,"
pp. 105-106.

Venice feared the growing power of Scanderbeg, who, like his father before him, had broken the Venetian economic monopoly over his lands. They watched with apprehension as Scanderbeg extended his domains at the expense of his neighbors and were concerned that he might try to take possession of their territories along the Adriatic coast,[76] of great importance to the maritime republic for strategic, as well as economic reasons.

The conflict between Scanderbeg and Venice erupted into war in 1447 when the Venetians seized the town of Dagno, a possession of Lek Zakarija, an Albanian noble and member of the league of Alessio. Zakarija had been killed in a feud with Lek Dukagjin and left no heirs. His lands were located between the Dukagjin territories and the coastal possessions of Venice, near Scutari. After his murder, Zakarija's mother invited the Venetians to take control of Dagno as an act of defiance toward the Dukagjins, who had killed her son.[77]

This behavior is quite understandable, especially in light of the tradition of the blood feud amongst the Albanians. This also drew Scanderbeg into the conflict. The Albanian leader, fearing the extension of Venetian influence in the country, contended that, as Zakarija had been a member

---

[76]Bicoku, "Quleques aspects," p. 98; Malltezi, "Le monopole," p. 139; and Ducellier, *L'Albanie*, p. 649.

[77]Moore, *George Castriot*, p. 77.

of the League of Alessio, Dagno should fall under its jurisdiction. This meant under his personal control. Scanderbeg
stated his case as follows: "There is not one of you who does
not know the hearty friendship that existed between me and
the elder Lek Zakarija, whose death has stirred everywhere
so many troubles. He and I had made with each other so
inviolable an agreement that whosoever of us two should
die first without issue, the survivor would inherit all his domains."[78]

Scanderbeg hoped to use the occasion of the conflict between Zakarija and the Dukagjins to further extend his
power, but Venetian intervention made this much more difficult. The seriousness of the situation led him to declare
war on the Republic in the spring of 1447.[79] In so doing, he
received support from most of the Albanian nobles who
feared an extension of the political and economic power of
the Republic of St. Mark in Albania.

Castriota may have decided to opt for a military solu-
tion to the dispute because during this time Venice was also
at war with Serbia over control of the Dalmatian coast, and
thus would be forced to divide her resources. He laid siege
to Dagno, but lacked the artillery necessary to destroy its
walls and take the city. The Venetians, realizing that they

---

[78]According to Barletti, translated in Drizari, *Scanderbeg*, p. 34.

[79]Moore, *George Castriot*, pp. 78-79; Frashëri, *History of Albania*, p. 73;
Knolles, *Generall Historie of the Turkes*, p. 311; and Radeshi, *Beteja e Drinit
dhe Oranikut*, an insightful monograph on the war between Scanderbeg
and the Venetians.

lacked a military force capable of taking the offensive against the Albanians, resorted to other tactics. In May of 1447 the Venetian Senate promised an annual pension of 100 ducats to an unnamed prominent Albanian who offered to assassinate Scanderbeg[80] – a plan which ultimately failed. As most members of the League appear to have remained loyal to him during the conflict with Venice, it is likely that the prominent Albanian referred to was one of the nobles upon whose domains Scanderbeg had already encroached. The war remained a stalemate until the summer of 1448. The Venetians maintained a defensive posture, while Scanderbeg lacked the heavy artillery necessary to batter the walls of the fortress and the manpower required to maintain a prolonged siege.

Meanwhile, having reestablished his control over the Empire, Sultan Murad II decided to take advantage of the war between Scanderbeg and Venice and personally lead an expedition into Albania to reestablish Ottoman authority there, a venture which the maritime republic encouraged.[81] This, of course, was not the only time the Venetians collaborated with the enemy of Christendom in pursuit of their own interests. Scanderbeg, aware of Ottoman intentions and expecting an imminent attack from the east, realized he

---

[80]Doc. 17 in Radonić, Gjuragj Kastrioti Skenderbeg, pp. 9-10. See also Radeshi Beteja e Drinit dhe Oranikut, pp. 14-15; and Marinesco, "Alphonse V," p. 31.

[81]Docs. 18 and 23 in Radonić, *Gjuragj Kastrioti Skenderbeg*, pp. 10-13 and 16-17; and Radeshi, *Beteja e Drinit dhe Oranikut*, p. 16.

needed to prepare for a two-front war; thus, in December 1447, he sent envoys across the Adriatic to the arch-rival of the Republic of St. Mark in Italy, Alphonso V, the King of Aragon, Sicily and Naples, to appeal for assistance.[82]

When spring arrived, the Sultan gathered his army and set out personally against Scanderbeg, his former servant turned rebel, who had repelled the previous Ottoman forces sent against him. In June, 1448, Murad's army laid siege to Sfietgrade on the eastern frontier of the Albanian territories under the control of the League. This fortress was of great strategic importance as it protected the easiest passage into the country from the east. Scanderbeg knew well the weapons and practices of the Ottoman army which began its campaign season in the spring and ended it in the fall, and made certain that all of his fortresses were not only strongly fortified to resist Ottoman artillery, but also well-provisioned to hold out against a prolonged siege by the enemy which, in any event, he knew would be lifted by late fall. Sfietgrade also had a great advantage because the surrounding forests and mountains made the approaches to the stronghold very difficult and rendered artillery virtually ineffective.[83]

While Scanderbeg was occupied with the war against the Venetians in the western part of the country, the fortress defiantly held out against a determined Ottoman siege.

---

[82]Marinesco, "Alphonse V," pp. 25-26; and Radeshi, *Beteja e Drinit dhe Oranikut*, p. 12.

[83]Moore, *George Castriot*, pp. 131, 154.

Meanwhile, on 23 July, Scanderbeg defeated a Venetian army in a battle along the Drin River.[84] After defeating the Venetians, he left part of his army, under the command of his nephew Hamsa, to lay siege to Dagno, while he began the arduous march across country to try to relieve the garrison at Sfietgrade. The entry of Naples into the war against Venice aided the Albanians in their two-front war.

Murad, anticipating the arrival of the Albanian leader, took the precaution of establishing a rear guard to protect the Ottoman forces from a surprise attack by the Albanians; thus, although Scanderbeg's forces inflicted heavy casualties upon the Ottomans, they failed to break the siege. Finally, in August, Sfietgrade surrendered to the Sultan after the city's water supply had been cut off and the well poisoned when an Ottoman spy tossed an animal carcass into it.[85] The Sultan, however, could not follow up his victory and lead his army west against Croya because he received word that John Hunyadi, the most dangerous of his enemies, was organizing another Balkan campaign. Thus, Mu-

---

[84]Radeshi, *Beteja e Drinit dhe Oranikut*, pp. 21-32; and Knolles, *Generall Historie of the Turkes*, p. 311.

[85]Moore, *George Castriot*, pp. 157-160; Oruc in *Burime osmane*, pp. 45-46 [f. 121]; and "Kronikat osmane anonime," in *Burime osmane*, pp. 55-56 [f. 70].

rad left a garrison in place to defend Sfietgrade and withdrew with his army to Adrianople to prepare for the Hungarian attack.[86]

Scanderbeg took advantage of this reprieve to conclude
the war with Venice. Realizing the increased Ottoman threat
after the loss of Sfietgrade and acknowledging his inability
to take the city, he signed a peace treaty with the Republic
of St. Mark on 4 October 1448 in which he ceded his rights
to Dagno in return for an annual pension of 1,400 ducats.[87]
Another reason that led him to renounce his claims to the
city was that Scanderbeg had been in contact with John
Hunyadi and had promised to join the Christian coalition
that was heading south through Serbia, something that he
could not risk doing before concluding the war at home.

Scanderbeg's efforts to unite with Christian force were
in vain. When the Albanians attempted to march into Serbian controlled territory, they found the mountain passes
blocked by the forces of the Serbian Prince George
Branković, whom Hunyadi had restored to the throne in
1443, but who now proved to be an important ally of the
Turkish Sultan. The result was a tragedy for the Christian
cause. The Ottomans decisively defeated Hunyadi's army,
which had managed to reach as far south as the Albanian

---

[86]Oruc in *Burime osmane*, p. 46 [f. 121].

[87]"Marrëveshja e paqes midis Lidhjes shqiptare dhe Republikës së
Venedikut," dok. 196 in *Burime të zgjedhura*, vol. II, pp. 296-297. An
outline of the treaty can be found in Radeshi, *Beteja e Drinit dhe Oranikut*,
pp. 44-45.

inhabited lands of Kosovo, on 19 October 1448, when Scanderbeg and his troops were still some thirty miles away.

After Hunyadi's defeat, Scanderbeg prepared himself for the inevitable Ottoman attack. It came in the spring of 1450 when Murad II, accompanied by his son Mehmed, invaded Albania with a force of over 100,000 men, determined to put an end to Scanderbeg's resistance once and for all. Against this massive invasion force Scanderbeg could only muster approximately 18,000 troops. The Albanians adopted a scorched-earth policy all along the Ottoman invasion route, as the peasants burned their fields and retreated into the mountains and forests. Bands of peasant soldiers ambushed and harassed the Ottoman forces all along the way to Croya, but the Ottomans were too powerful to be stopped. On 14 May 1450, the Sultan's army appeared before the walls of Croya. Scanderbeg had left a garrison of 1,500 men under the command of Count Uran, one of his ablest officers, to defend the city, while he withdrew with the remainder of his troops into the mountains to the north of the fortress.

Murad tried bribes and threats to get the loyal defenders of Croya to capitulate, but it was to no avail. The siege continued into the summer. A letter, dated 13 August 1450, from the Senate of Ragusa to John Hunyadi, the Governor of Hungary, reveals the situation at the time: "The Turkish Emperor, together with his son [Mehmed II], maintains a very strong army in the lands of Albania and has pitched its tents in front of Croya, the city of Scanderbeg, and attempts

VARNA TVVM ILLVSTRAT SVPERATO PANONE NOMEN
HÆC TIBI SED CHRISTO VINDICE FAMA VENIT.

SVLTAN AMV RAT CHAN

56

VEXAT TE IMPOSTOR DVSMES.QVEM INFIDA TVORVM
TVRBA INSPERATA PRODITIONE IVVAT.

B 2

Sultan Murad II

with all his might and vigorous battle to crush him. Therefore, after they pitched their tents against this city, he [Mu-
rad II] gave an order that two bombards be cast from metals
that they had brought with them for this purpose, the big-
gest of which, according to the information that we have received, can launch stone projectiles weighing 400 pounds.
Nevertheless, the city is fortified with all the materials that
are needed for its defense and preservation, and the land
itself cannot be easily taken under control because of its
harsh and difficult nature. Inside the city there are 1,500 bat-
tle-tested men. For this reason, it is believed that the Turkish
Army is wasting its time trying to conquer this city as the
brave men inside are bound by honor to defend it to the
death. Scanderbeg himself is not far from the Turkish tents
and daily inflicts heavy losses on the enemy because he
takes advantage of the nature of the country and the nearby
mountains where he hides without being discovered. If we
receive any further news that will be of value to you, we will
endeavor to keep your majesty informed."[88]

The fact that Ottoman artillery could not maintain a
steady bombardment allowed the Albanians in the city to
repair the damage inflicted on the walls before it became too
serious. As the Ottomans pillaged the countryside and cut

---

[88]"Nga letra që Senati I Raguzës I dërgon guvernatorit të Hungarisë
Janosh Huniadit," dok. 198 in *Burime të zgjedhura*, vol. II, p. 197. On this
siege see also "Rrethimi I Krujës," dok. 200 in *Burime të zgjedhura*, vol. II,
pp. 298-307; and Jovius, *A Short Treatise upon the Turkes Chronicles*,
fol. XXII.

off water and provisions to the beleaguered citadel, the situation became desperate. Meanwhile, Scanderbeg's forces continued to harass the Ottoman troops from the rear, occasionally inflicting heavy losses on the invaders, especially when one of their detachments strayed from the main army, but it was not enough to force the Sultan to raise the siege.

Complicating his situation, Scanderbeg faced serious political problems internally, as members of the League of Alessio began to secede from the alliance. As Ottoman success appeared more likely with every passing day, many Albanian nobles began to make peace with the Sultan in hopes of retaining their lands and titles. Others welcomed the invader because they wanted to break the power which Scanderbeg had accumulated during the first six years of the revolt and which he had used against many of them. Some hoped the Sultan would restore the balance of power that had characterized the Albanian aristocracy before the formation of the League of Alessio. Only those nobles serving in Scanderbeg's army remained loyal throughout the siege.

The Venetians also dealt a heavy blow to Scanderbeg's position by provisioning the Ottoman forces. A Venetian report from the time of the invasion bears witness to this: "We received a letter from Albania on 13 September informing us that the Turks have pitched their tents against Croya and that Scanderbeg is defending himself heroically. If the count of Shkodra had not supplied flour and fresh bread to the Turks, the latter would have pulled up their tents; for this reason, it is feared that Scanderbeg, the moment he frees himself [of the Turks] will attack the lands of the Republic."[89]

Venetian supplies were critical to the Ottomans because the Albanians had destroyed the surrounding lands and Scanderbeg's forces continually disrupted their supply lines from the east.

By autumn the situation was critical for both sides. Even with Venetian help, the Ottomans had a difficult time supplying their large army and the approaching winter would amplify this problem, leaving them under-provisioned and vulnerable in the mountains. The Albanians also suffered from a shortage of manpower and supplies. It took all the resources which Scanderbeg could muster to resist the Ottomans; the League of Alessio had dissolved, but Scanderbeg's forces both inside and outside the citadel continued their resistance through sheer will and determination.

Sultan Murad maintained the siege for as long as possible, but with the harsh winter rapidly approaching, he realized that he would have to withdraw. An anonymous Ottoman chronicle from the time describes the Sultan's decision to abandon the siege: "They struck Croya with cannons and turned it into a graveyard. He hoped that they would surrender, but they did not. Winter then arrived. The commanders said, 'Let us attack!' But the Sultan said to them: 'If we attack many of our men will be killed. I would not give

---

[89]"Nga analet e Venedikut," dok. 199 in *Burime të zgjedhura*, vol. II, p. 298; and doc. 35 in Radonić, *Gjuragj Kastriot Skenderbeg*, p. 20.

the life of even one brave man for fifty fortresses such as this.'"[90] On 26 October 1450, the Ottoman army began the long retreat eastward. It had been a costly campaign for both sides. Dismayed by his lack of success against Scanderbeg, Murad returned to Adrianople where he died some months later.

The Ottomans left Albania a devastated land. Homes and crops had been burned and famine threatened during the winter. Abandoned by most of the Albanian nobility, many assumed that Scanderbeg had been defeated, but he had created an army directly loyal to him. He had also cultivated the support of the peasants and so, in this time of desperation, he had a base of power to fall back on. Indeed, the siege of Croya in 1450 marks a turning point in the Albanian revolt under the leadership of Scanderbeg. Although he had been undermining the League of Alessio from the moment he began organizing his army in 1444, it had continued to function, such as during the conflict with Venice after the death of Lek Zakarija. Now it was a dead issue. After he successfully resisted the Ottoman attack, despite being abandoned by a large part of his League allies, it was clear that this organization no longer represented the basis of Scanderbeg's power. The real authority and power in Albania lay in the hands of the son of John Castriota, and he would use it against those who had betrayed him in his moment of need.

---

[90]"Kronikat osmane anonime," in *Burime osmane*, p. 56 [f. 73].

Chapter V
The Revolt of the Masses

"'Rise like Lions after slumber
In unvanquishable number -
Shake your chains to earth like dew
Which in sleep had fallen on you -
Ye are many - they are few.'"

— *Percy Bysshe Shelley*, The Mask of Anarchy[91]

The moral victory of holding out against the massive Ottoman invasion force created a sense of euphoria which, despite the high cost of the victory, spread throughout the mountains of Albania and into the rest of Europe. Scanderbeg received food, weapons, financial assistance, and the materials to repair his battered fortresses, along with congratulations from Pope Nicholas V, who hailed him as a Champion of Christendom, as well as King Ladislas of Hungary, Philip the Good, Duke of Burgundy, and Alphonso V. Several adventurers from France and Germany came to join

---

[91]Shelley, "The Mask of Anarchy," stanza XCI, in *Shelley Poetical Works*, p. 344.

the army of the mighty Scanderbeg,[92] who was already becoming legendary throughout Europe. With the support of his army, Scanderbeg directed the reconstruction of Albania and rapidly restored order in his lands.

Realizing the need for greater resources to continue his defiance of the Sultan, Scanderbeg began to seek outside assistance through diplomatic channels. He sent envoys, along with a gift of six Turkish prisoners of war, to Philip the Good of Burgundy to encourage the Duke, who had long supported the idea of a crusade against the Turks, to organize such an effort.[93] The most significant assistance came from directly across the sea. On 26 March 1451 Scanderbeg signed a treaty of alliance with King Alphonso V of Naples, who had supported him in his conflict with Venice three years earlier. The fact that both leaders shared common enemies in Venice and the Sultan drew them together. In return for recognizing Alphonso's suzerainty, Scanderbeg received an annual pension of 1,500 ducats, along with food, weapons, and 100 Catalan soldiers, as well as materials and workmen to help repair the battered walls of Croya.[94]

---

[92]Moore, *George Castriot*, pp. 168, 210; Babinger, *Mehmed the Conqueror*, p. 61; Setton, *Papacy and the Levant*, vol. II, p. 102; Armstrong, *Heroes of Defeat*, pp. 227-228; and Gibbon, *Decline and Fall of the Roman Empire*, vol. III, p. 742.

[93]Vaughan, *Europe and the Turk*, p. 70.

[94]"Traktati i Gaetës midis Alfonsit të Napolit dhe Skenderbeut," dok. 203 in *Burime të zgjedhura*, vol. II, pp. 308-310.

Improving his defensive fortifications was one of the principal problems Scanderbeg needed to address following the invasion of 1450. His new alliance with Naples assisted him in these endeavors. Barletti recounts the rebuilding of Croya after the siege of 1450: "While Mahomet [Mehmed II] was establishing himself on the throne of his ancestors, the Prince of Epire [Scanderbeg] was engaged in repairing the ruins of Croya. He entirely renewed the old fortifications, which were in dilapidated condition, partly from the effects of time, and partly from the cannon of the enemy. He added other defenses of a more modern description, and not like those which were constructed before the use of ordnance, when the chief security of cities consisted in the valor of those who defended them. Among the new fortifications of Croya, Scanderbeg caused a large and strong tower to be built at the city gate, decreasing gradually in circumference as it rose. The other parts of the town were strengthened by works constructed under the direction of able engineers."[95] The new walls were rounded so as to better absorb the impact of cannon fire which was becoming more powerful and accurate during this period.

The Albanian leader also sought to hinder the entry of the Ottoman armies into his lands. According to Barletti: "In Lower Dibra he observed a pass through which, as being the most convenient, the Turks had ever been accustomed to in-

---

[95]Moore, *George Castriot*, p. 211.

vade his territories, and make sudden inroads for the purpose of foraging or of laying waste the country... Near this pass was a rugged mountain called Modrissa, of great height, from the top of which the frontiers of the enemy might be seen for a great distance. On the summit of this mountain, he resolved to build a fort, whose cannon might give notice to the neighboring country of the approach of the Turks, and which might also, in case of need, afford a place of refuge for the inhabitants in its vicinity... In pursuance of this design he speedily returned to Croya, whose fortifications were now complete, and took thence a number of masons, carpenters and other workmen... With this band, he proceeded to Modrissa and engaged in the work with so much diligence that it was finished without any annoyance from the Turks.... The fortress of Modrissa in less than six months was enclosed and encompassed with walls, and provided with accommodations for the soldiers. The place was so strong by nature that it required no ditches or ramparts."[96] The construction of this border outpost again reflects one of the defensive principles applied so effectively by the Albanian leader – the skillful use of the natural terrain in conjunction with man-made fortifications.

The alliance with Scanderbeg was one in a series of treaties which the Neapolitan King concluded with Christian

---

[96]Moore, *George Castriot*, pp. 212-214.

rulers in the Balkans during this time.[97] Alphonso envisioned himself at the head of a great crusade to drive the Ottomans out of southeastern Europe and to establish himself as the Emperor of a new Roman Empire.[98] These dreams were probably quite vivid in light of the news that Sultan Murad II had died the month before and was succeeded by his young son, Mehmed II, who had proven unable to maintain order in the Empire during Murad's brief retirement only a few years earlier. In return for much needed material support that he received, Scanderbeg gave up very little, recognizing only nominal Neapolitan suzerainty. In accordance with the terms of the treaty, he did not have to pay tribute or homage to his new suzerain until after the Ottomans were driven from Europe.[99]

Having gained a powerful foreign sponsor, Scanderbeg now began to take his revenge upon those who had betrayed him during the Ottoman siege of Croya. After the League had fallen apart, there was nothing to restrain Scanderbeg in his attempts to extend his control over the lands of neighboring lords so his actions against them became

---

[97]For example, he also concluded a treaty with George Araniti, see "Traktati midis Alfonsit të Napolit dhe Gjergj Arianitit," dok. 204 in *Burime të zgjedhura*, vol. II, pp. 310-312.

[98]Marinesco, "Alphonse V," pp. 44-45.

[99]"Traktati I Gaetës midis Alfonsit të Napolit dhe Skenderbeut," in dok. 203 in *Burime të zgjedhura*, vol. II, pp. 208-210.

more pronounced. He annexed their lands and placed garrisons loyal to him in their fortresses. In addition, he dis-
missed inefficient officers from his army and replaced them
with others selected on the basis of their ability and personal
loyalty.

A contemporary to these events, the Albanian nobleman John Muzaka, described Scanderbeg's policy: 'He took
the decision to get hold of all the country [from the other
nobles]... He put in jail the lords Gjon and Gajko Balsha...
and seized their estate, which was situated between Croya
and Alessio; from the lord Moisi Komneni, he seized his estate, which was in Dibra... And after my father had died, he
took from us Tomorica and Myzeqe Vogel, and in the same
way he dealt with other lords also, but they could do nothing, for he had the army in his hands and they had perpet-
ually the Turks at their back."[100]

Yet Scanderbeg was still unable to deal with two of the
most powerful Albanian nobles, George Araniti and Nicholas Dukagjin, both of whom had abandoned him during the
siege of Croya, in a like way. In April, 1451, he resolved his
differences with Araniti by marrying his daughter Donika,
thus concluding an alliance between the two families.[101] The

---

[100]"Tradhëtia feudale sipas bujarit Gjon Muzaka, 1455-1457," dok. 208 in
Burime të zgjedhura, vol. II, p. 315.

[101]Moore, *George Castriot*, p. 211; Gegaj, *L'Albanie et l'invasion turque*,
p. 51; Drizari, *Scanderbeg*, p. 43; and Paganel, *Histoire de Scanderbeg*, p.
142.

peace between the two Albanian leaders was probably facilitated by Alphonso V who became their suzerain that same
year.

This secured Scanderbeg's southern border, but a reso-
lution of his conflict with the Dukagjins to his north proved
more difficult as they sought Ottoman support to offset his
power that had increased following his alliances with Naples and the Aranitis. The conflict between Castriota and the
Dukagjins lasted until 1454 when Pope Nicholas V inter-
vened and mediated a peace agreement between the two Albanian nobles.[102]

Scanderbeg's difficulties with Venice continued as the
maritime republic, which had provisioned the Ottoman invaders during the siege of Croya, now refused to abide by
the terms of the peace treaty of 1448 and pay his annual pension. Venice had attempted to stir up opposition amongst
the Albanian nobility during and after the siege of Croya in
hopes of diminishing his power – a threat to their economic
interests and coastal possessions in Albania. Their efforts
failed, however, and, following negotiations between them
and Scanderbeg's new ally, Alphonso V, they agreed to re-
sume payment of the pension in 1453.[103]

Within a year after the near disaster at Croya, Scanderbeg emerged more powerful than ever before. Any hopes

---

[102]Pastor, *History of the Popes*, vol. II, p. 430.

[103]"Marrëdhëniet e Skendërbeut më Republikën e Venedikut," dok. 205
in *Burime të zgjedhura*, vol. II, pp. 312-313.

Scanderbeg's wife Donika Araniti Castriota

that the death of Sultan Murad II in February, 1451 might weaken the Ottoman Empire and make it vulnerable to a Christian offensive were soon dashed as young Mehmed II proved to be much more adept than his previous brief reign had indicated, and now set out on a policy to consolidate the Empire south of the Danube.

To accomplish this objective, the young Sultan had to deal with obstacles posed by Albania, Hungary, Serbia, Wallachia, Moldavia, and Byzantium, as well as revolts in the Morea. With this goal in mind, Mehmed sent two expeditions into Albania in 1452. Each took a separate invasion route, but planned to join together in an attack on Croya. Scanderbeg received intelligence information about the Ottoman strategy and rushed to meet each of the Turkish forces separately, before they could unite. On 21 July, the Albanians defeated one of the Ottoman armies at Modrica, and captured their commander Hamza Pasha. Scanderbeg then proceeded to intercept the second invasion force, which he defeated in battle on the Mechadi plain, killing the Turkish commander. After this success, he ransomed Hamza Pasha to Sultan Mehmed II who paid the substantial sum of 13,000 ducats for his safe return. Scanderbeg then distributed the money amongst his soldiers.[104]

The next Ottoman invasion came in the spring of 1453 when the Albanians defeated an Ottoman expeditionary

---

[104]Moore, *George Castriot*, pp. 218-219; Knolles, *Generall Historie of the Turkes*, pp. 365-366; *George Kastriot-Scanderbeg and the Albanian-Turkish War*, p. 86; and Armstrong, *Heroes of Defeat*, pp. 229-230.

force of 14,000 men in the Pallogu plain between Dibra and Tetova.[105] Mehmed undoubtedly realized that these smaller forces had little hope of defeating Scanderbeg's army which had withstood the long siege of Murad's massive invasion force in 1450, but he wanted to keep pressure on the Albanians and gradually weaken their resistance by pillaging the land. During the early years of his reign, Mehmed directed most of his attention to the conquest of Byzantium, and to putting down a revolt of Albanians in the Morea who may have been inspired by Scanderbeg's success.[106]

After the fall of Constantinople in 1453, the Sultan devoted a great deal of his energy and resources to rebuilding the city and making it the new capital of his Empire. The fall of Constantinople stunned Christian Europe and caused a panic in political circles throughout most of the continent. Alphonso V's policy turned defensive as he feared an Ottoman invasion of Italy. Scanderbeg became an especially significant part of this policy because, for strategic and tactical reasons, control of Albania would be a necessary prerequisite for a Turkish advance across the Adriatic into southern Italy, less than fifty miles away. Alphonso hoped to make the mountains of Albania an advance line of defense for his

---

[105]Knolles, *Generall Historie of the Turkes*, pp. 366-367.

[106]Miller, *Essays on the Latin Orient*, p. 103.

kingdom, thus he increased his financial support to Scanderbeg by an additional 1,500 ducats annually.[107] In addition, the Neapolitan King urged Pope Nicholas V to send Scanderbeg 1,000 infantrymen and 200 cavalrymen,[108] but Papal support was strictly limited due to financial difficulties and Italian concerns. Venice also began to fear the growing Ottoman threat after the fall of Constantinople and agreed to unite its forces in Albania under Scanderbeg's command, but this plan was never carried out because the Republic of St. Mark signed a new peace accord with Mehmed II in April, 1454, establishing commercial and diplomatic relations with the Ottoman Empire.[109]

In 1455, Mehmed the Conqueror undertook a campaign against Serbia, attempting to bring the principality again under direct Ottoman rule. Scanderbeg took advantage of the situation and went on the offensive, leading his 14,000-man army to Berat, a fortress in southern Albania under Ottoman control. The alliance with Aranitis, whose lands lay between his and the Turkish controlled territory to the south, made it possible for Scanderbeg to attempt to weaken

---

[107]Moore, *George Castriot*, p. 233; Marinesco, "Alfonse V," p. 75; *George Kastriot-Scanderbeg and the Albanian-Turkish War*, p. 87; and Vaughan, *Europe and the Turk*, p. 74.

[108]Ryder, *The Kingdon of Naples under Alphonso the Magnanimous*, p. 267.

[109]Marinesco, "Alphonse V," pp. 74-76; and *George Kastriot-Scanderbeg and the Albanian-Turkish War*, p. 87.

the Ottoman grip on that region. The Albanians received active support from Alphonso V who sent 1,000 men and twelve cannon to participate in the expedition against Berat.[110]

After a short siege during June and July, the fortress was ready to capitulate to the Albanians, but then, suddenly, an Ottoman army of as many as 40,000 men attacked Scanderbeg's army from the rear. This assault had taken him by surprise. Moisi Golemi, his trusted general assigned to protect the eastern border, had betrayed him and allowed the Ottomans to pass into Albania without his commander's knowledge. As a result, the Albanians were defeated by the Ottoman forces on 26 July 1455, losing almost 5,000 men in the battle before retreating northward into the mountains.[111]

Encouraged by the Venetians, several nobles turned against Scanderbeg, thinking that the defeat at Berat had diminished his power, but the Albanian leader quickly replenished his army before they or the Ottomans could capitalize on his misfortune.[112] The defection of Moisi Golemi to the

---

[110]Thiriet, "Quelques reflexions sur la politique venetienne à l'egad de Georges Skanderbeg," p. 91 ; Noli, *George Castrioti Scanderbeg*, p. 50 ; and Setton, *Papacy and the Levant*, vol. II, p. 192, who states that Alphonso intended to send more troops, but was unable to do so because of Italian concerns.

[111]"Dok. 209, Beteja e Beratit," in *Burime të zgjedhura*, vol. II, pp. 315-316; and Knolles, *Generall Historie of the Turkes*, pp. 368-371.

[112]Gegaj, *L'Albanie et l'invasion turque*, p. 56 ; and Noli, *George Castrioti Scanderbeg*, p. 51.

Ottomans in 1455 demonstrates the extent to which Scanderbeg impinged upon the territories of other Albanian nobles. Golemi, one of Scanderbeg's most capable officers, had served loyally since the organization of the League of Alessio. After 1451, when Scanderbeg amplified his centralization efforts, he began to impose his control even over the lands of loyal nobles – a policy he justified by the need to organize the country's resources efficiently to meet the Ottoman threat. The Sultan had promised Golemi a large pension and freedom to rule over all of his hereditary lands if he helped the Ottomans defeat Scanderbeg.

While Mehmed II occupied himself with the unsuccessful siege of Belgrade in 1456, valiantly defended by John Hunyadi, Moisi Golemi led an Ottoman force of approximately 15,000 men into Albania. Scanderbeg, who had received advance information about the invasion route and the strength of the Turkish forces, crushed the invaders in a battle near Dibra. Moisi escaped, but soon after he returned to Scanderbeg and asked forgiveness for his treason. Scanderbeg responded by pardoning Golemi and restored his lands and former rank to him. Moisi served his commander loyally for the remainder of his life.[113] Considering Scanderbeg's benevolent treatment of his treacherous comrade, it is quite possible that the two had come to terms before the invasion in 1456 and that it may have been Golemi himself

---

[113]On the defection of Golemi, see Moore, *George Castriot*, pp. 232-233 and 251-269; Pastor, *History of the Popes*, vol. II, p. 432; and Knolles, *General Historie of the Turkes*, pp. 372-374.

who informed him of the invasion plan, leading the Turkish forces into an ambush.

Moisi Golemi was not the only one of his officers to betray Scanderbeg. That same year, 1456, one of Scanderbeg's nephews, George Balsha, turned over the fortress of Modritza to an Ottoman garrison as an act of protest against his uncle's infringement of the rights and territories of his family. The efforts of these nobles to stop the growth of Scanderbeg's power can be attributed to the fact that he had become too strong for them to successfully oppose him without outside assistance. Thus, they appealed to the Sultan as the Ottomans alone could muster a military force capable of confronting the Albanian leader.

At the end of 1456 Scanderbeg's only son, whom he named after his father, was born. Before the birth of John, Scanderbeg's nephew Hamsa, whom the Albanian leader had once referred to as "my chief friend and counsellor and the faithful companion of my travels"[114] had been his heir; the prospect of losing his inheritance, which he himself had helped to build and felt rightly belonged to him, fighting at his uncle's side since the beginning of the revolt, led Hamsa to defect to the Ottomans. According to the Ottoman chronicler Ashik Pashazade: "there came to him [the Sultan], from the Albanian lands, Hamsa Beg, the nephew of Scanderbeg and he said to him: 'My Sultan, in the Albanian lands many

---

[114]According to Barletti, quoted in Drizari, *Scanderbeg*, p. 2.

Scanderbeg's nephew Hamsa

people have become enemies of Scanderbeg. If you command me, my Sultan, I will go and conquer Croya.' The Sultan informed the pashas of this proposal. The pashas replied
to the Sultan: 'We are in agreement, our Sultan, send him.'
He then prepared what was needed for the military expedition."[115]

The Sultan had promised to make him Governor of Albania if he could defeat his uncle; this was enough to per-
suade Hamsa to lead a large Ottoman military force of as
many as 80,000 troops, together with Isak bey Evrenos, into
Albania in the summer of 1457. Scanderbeg retreated before
the invaders and did not engage the enemy in battle; while
the Ottomans ravaged the countryside, the Albanian army
gathered in the mountains and waited for the opportunity
to launch a counterattack in favorable conditions. Due to the
lack of resistance encountered, the Ottomans, led by Hamsa,
believed that Scanderbeg was defeated and abandoned by
the population and grew increasingly confident of their success. It was not to be, however, for, on 7 September 1457,
Scanderbeg launched a surprise counter-attack, defeating
the Ottomans decisively, killing or capturing over half of the
Turkish forces. Among the prisoners was his traitorous

---

[115]"Dok. 213, Tradhëtia e Hamza Kastriotit," in *Burime të zgjedhura*,
vol. II, p. 318. This document provides another indication of the growing
discontent among Albanian nobles faced with Scanderbeg's efforts at
centralization.

nephew, Hamsa, whom he sent to King Alphonso.[116] Scanderbeg later pardoned his nephew. A secret staged prison escape was arranged and Hamsa fled to Constantinople to serve as a spy for the Albanian leader. Unfortunately for Hamsa, the Porte soon discovered the ruse and he was promptly executed.[117]

Scanderbeg's fame increased after the victory of 1457, but little foreign aid was forthcoming. The Pope could offer little more than verbal support when the Albanian leader appealed to him for material assistance to continue his war against the Turks; Calixtus III wrote to Scanderbeg in September, 1457: "Beloved son! Continue to defend the Catholic faith; God, for whom you fight, will not abandon his cause. He will, I am confident, grant success against the Turks and the other unbelievers to you and the rest of the Christians with glory and honor."[118] Only nominal material support, in the form of fifty soldiers, was received from the Philip the

---

[116]On the defection of Hamsa, see Moore, *George Castriot*, pp. 270-285, 290; and Knolles, *Generall Historie of the Turkes*, pp. 375, 382-383. On the Ottoman campaign in Albania in 1457 see Oruc, Burime osmane, p. 46 [f. 72]; "Dok. 216, Markezi de Vareze në Venedik e njofton Dukën e Milanos, 2 gusht 1457; Dok 218, Turqit kremtojnë në Albulenë fitoren mbi Skenderbeun; Dok. 220, Kardinali Solvio Enea Pikolomini i shkruan Martin Majerit mbi katastrofën e turqve në Shqipëri, 1457," in *Burime të zgjedhura*, vol. II, pp. 320-321.

[117]Knolles, *Generall Historie of the Turkes*, pp. 382-383; and Moore *George Castriot*, pp. 295-296.

[118]Quoted in Pastor, *History of the Popes*, vol. II, p. 434.

Good,[119] who probably dreamed about an anti-Ottoman crusade more than anyone else in western Europe, but for one reason or another could never quite turn the dream into reality. The greatest blow to Scanderbeg's efforts against the Turks came in 1458, with the death of his suzerain King Alphonso. The Neapolitan King had been the his most reliable source of material support, especially since the collapse of the League of Alessio following Murad's expedition in 1450.

After the unsuccessful invasion of Albania in 1457, the Ottomans were occupied with revolts in the Morea and completing the conquest of Serbia. In 1459, they again turned their attention to Albania when Mehmed II sent a force, once more led by Isak bey Evrenos, to pillage the countryside at harvest time and burn the crops.[120] The reasons the Turks adopted this strategy were twofold. First, they wanted to make the population suffer for their resistance to Ottoman authority. Secondly, they hoped to destroy Scanderbeg's grain export, his largest source of revenue to finance his war against them.[121]

In 1461, Mehmed II decided to settle the situation in Europe so that he could concentrate on problems which had arisen in Anatolia where revolts against Ottoman authority

---

[119]Gegaj, *L'Albanie et l'invasion turque*, p. 111.

[120]Kritovoulos, *History of Mehmed the Conqueror*, pp. 146-147 [III,96]; and Oruc in *Burime osmane*, p. 47 [f. 125].

[121]Hrabak, "Exportations de cereales," p. 112.

had broken out. Albania was among the last outposts of resistance to Ottoman rule in the Balkans and Mehmed had already expended great resources in unsuccessful attempts to subdue the land. Thus, in the summer of 1461, Mehmed offered Scanderbeg a three-year truce.[122] In considering the Sultan's proposal, the Albanian leader sent envoys to Pope Pius II to inform the pontiff of the Sultan's offer and to ascertain if aid from the Christian powers of Europe would be forthcoming in the aftermath of the Congress of Mantua. The Pope replied: "My dear son, we answer that the Roman Catholic Pontiff does not give permission to anyone to make a treaty with the Infidels. There can be no agreement with them without offending God. We informed your spokesman that to send a legate to take your place and to defend your territories would not be of any help for the purpose requested because it is not an easy matter for us on account of our lack of power."[123]

Despite the Papal admonitions, the Albanians needed a respite. For nearly two decades the country had suffered almost yearly attacks and its resources were gradually being drained. With little prospect of foreign support, despite the new Pope's determined efforts to organize a great crusade, Scanderbeg could foresee no advantage in continuing the

---

[122]Knolles, *Generall Historie of the Turkes*, p. 386; Frashëri, *History of Albania*, p. 81; and *George Kastriot-Scanderbeg and the Albanian-Turkish War*, p. 96.

[123]Quoted in Drizari, *Scanderbeg*, p. 60.

conflict with the Turks. The country needed time to recover from the devastation of war. The prospect of peace with the Turks also suited Scanderbeg's political interests as it allowed him to send a cavalry force to Italy to support Alphonso's son, Ferrante, who was being challenged for the Neapolitan throne by the Angevins.

After concluding the armistice treaty with the Sultan, Scanderbeg personally led a force of two to three thousand troops across the Adriatic Sea to Italy in support of Ferrante, arriving there in August, 1461.[124] His reasons for intervention in the Italian conflict are clear. He had received his only significant foreign assistance from Naples, and he hoped that this aid would be resumed if Ferrante succeeded in establishing himself on the throne. On the other hand, an Angevin victory in Naples would have shifted the political focus of the southern Italian Kingdom toward France and the north. Scanderbeg explained his purpose for undertaking the expedition in Italy in a letter to the Prince of Taranto: "Alphonso sent me aid against the Turks when I was in dire straits. I should be ungrateful indeed if I did not do as much for his son."[125]

Scanderbeg won two important battles in Italy, one at Barletta and the other at Trani, which helped Ferrante establish his authority over Naples. Pope Pius II described the Albanian forces: "This cavalry, who were lightly armed,

---

[124]Pastor, *History of the Popes*, vol. III, p. 113.

[125]Quoted in Pius II, "The Commentaries of Pius II: Books VI-IX," p. 459.

mounted on swift horses, and accustomed to hardships, left nothing unharmed in the wide, level province. No herds could be hidden so far off that they could not find them in a single day's riding."[126] In appreciation for his help, Ferrante granted Castriota fiefs in his Kingdom and gave him an annual pension of 1,200 ducats. Scanderbeg had succeeded in assuring himself of renewed Neapolitan support, but Naples had been weakened by the dynastic struggle, thus prohibiting Ferrante from offering the Albanian leader the same level of financial and material support that his father had provided.

Meanwhile, Mehmed had his attention drawn back toward Europe when Vlad III Dracula, the Prince of Wallachia at the time, refused to pay the required tribute and initiated an offensive, attacking Turkish positions along the Danube during the winter of 1461-1462. The insolence of the Romanian prince led the Sultan to undertake a difficult, but suc

---

[126]Pius II, "The Commentaries of Pius II, Books VI-IX," p. 458. Despite this description, the Pope went on to erroneously claim that the Albanian cavalry, called the *Stradiots*, was ineffective in Italian warfare. Ferrante clearly acknowledged the importance of the Albanian forces, rewarding Scanderbeg handsomely. The Albanian cavalry became renowned throughout Europe in the fifteenth and sixteenth centuries, see Gibbon, *Decline and Fall of the Roman Empire*, vol. III, p. 743; and Hobhouse, *A Journey through Albania*, p. 155. Fan Noli, in his introduction to Faik Konitza's book, *Albania, the Rock Garden of Southeastern Europe*, commented that "in the sixteenth century when the French wanted to praise a horseman, they would say '*Il chevauche comme un Albanais*,'" p. XIX.

Pope Pius II

cessful campaign in the summer of 1462 that renewed Ottoman suzerainty over Wallachia and ousted the disloyal Vlad
from the throne, replacing him with his brother Radu the
Handsome. With Mehmed campaigning in Europe, Scanderbeg left Italy and returned to Albania to defend against
a possible Ottoman attack. During August and September
of 1463, Mehmed sent three small expeditions into Albania,
each of which met with defeat at the hands of Scanderbeg's
forces, but not before inflicting serious losses and damage
to the crops. This new outbreak of hostilities was short-lived
as representatives of Scanderbeg and the Sultan negotiated
a ten-year peace agreement at Shkup in April, 1463, much
to the dismay of Pope Pius II who continued to hope that a
great crusade against the Turkish Infidels would materialize. A political realist, Scanderbeg put no hope in empty
promises of western assistance; since Mehmed's peace proposal did not seek to impose any tribute and merely confirmed the political and military status quo, it was only logical that he should accept it. He could no longer carry on the
war alone.

Nevertheless, the ten-year peace accord between Scanderbeg and the Ottomans ended less than six months after
it was signed. In September, 1463, war broke out between
the Ottomans and the Venetians over control of several islands in the Aegean Sea. Pope Pius II took advantage of the
situation to try to put into action his beloved plan for a
Christian crusade against the Ottomans; the Pope hoped to
use revenues from newly discovered alum mines in church

lands to finance the expedition. The Pontiff's plan called for Scanderbeg to spearhead the Christian attack: "Scanderbeg and a very strong force of Albanians will join an army of 88,000... and many all over Greece will desert from the enemy."[127]

The Albanian leader was apprehensive about the crusade, having witnessed so many other failed efforts, and requested that he be granted refuge in Church lands should it fail;[128] at the same time, he realized that the geopolitical situation of his lands, being trapped between the Ottomans and the Venetians, left him no way to avoid being drawn into the conflict between the two great Levantine powers. With the Pope's intercession, Scanderbeg concluded an alliance with his old nemesis Venice in the fall of 1463. By the terms of the treaty he received financial and military support from both the Venetians and the Papacy, and his son John was made a citizen of Venice and granted the right of membership in the Grand Council.[129] Thus, in November, 1463, the Albanians, led by Scanderbeg, renewed their war against the Ottomans.

---

[127]Pius II, "The Commentaries of Pius II, Books II and III," p, 778.

[128]Pius II, "The Commentaries of Pius II, Books X-XIII,"pp. 806, 816. To encourage support for the crusade, the Pope planned for the division of Ottoman territory. Scanderbeg was to receive Macedonia.

[129]"Dok. 231, Marrëveshja midis Senatit të Venedikut dhe Skenderbeut, 20 gusht 1463," in Burime të zgjedhura, vol. II, pp. 333-336; Skendi, "Complex Environment," p. 175; Gegaj, L'Albanie et l'invasion turque, p. 135; and Frashëri, Scanderbeg, p. 34.

Unfortunately for the Albanians, Pius II's grand plan for a holy crusade against Turkish Infidels received little support in Europe. A major blow to the Christian cause was dealt when the King of France dissuaded Philip the Good of Burgundy, who was about to fulfill his long-cherished dream of personally leading an army of crusaders against the Sultan in the winter of 1463, from leaving so that he would be able to assist in case of hostilities with England.[130] Other European powers considered the crusade as only being beneficial to the Venetians, despite the Pope's appeals to the contrary, and wanted no part of it. The final blow came on 15 August 1464 when Pius II died at Ancona while organizing the papal forces destined to participate in his holy mission.[131] As Pius had been the spirit behind the idea of a great anti-Ottoman crusade, the dream died with him. Europeans, who would soon begin traveling westward across the ocean, turned their backs on the east, leaving Scanderbeg alone with the Venetians to oppose the Ottomans.

In August, 1464, Albanian forces repulsed an Ottoman invasion led by a renegade Albanian nobleman, Ballaban Pasha, but, in pursuit of the fleeing Turks, several of Scanderbeg's top officers, including Moisi Golemi, were captured. Although he tried to ransom them from the Sultan,

---

[130]Vaughan, *Philip the Good*, pp. 369-370.

[131] Pastor, *History of the Popes*, vol. III, p. 370; and Simonde de Sismondi, *A History of the Italian Republics*, p. 251.

Mehmed refused and ordered that they be executed,[132] thereby dealing a severe blow to the Albanians who lost some of their ablest commanders. Mehmed II probably decided not to abide by the customary practice of allowing the enemy to ransom high-ranking officials because he wanted to punish the Albanians for breaking the peace accord and joining the Venetians in their war against the Ottomans.

Early in 1465, Mehmed sent two spies into Albania with orders to assassinate Scanderbeg, but they were discovered before they could carry out their plan and summarily executed.[133] That same year Ballaban Pasha again led three separate expeditions against Scanderbeg, each of which was defeated and driven back by the Albanians; nevertheless, the last of these invasions inflicted great damage as it occurred at harvest time and destroyed much of the crop for that year.

Famine threatened during the winter and Albanian resources began to run low. While Scanderbeg had valiantly resisted Ottoman domination, the cost had been great; population decline hampered both the economy and the war effort, and Ottoman raids had devastated the land. Papal support, promised by Pius II, did not materialize after his death as the new Pope, Paul II, had little interest in crusading. King Ferrante could offer little assistance due the instability of his own Kingdom, and the Venetians were, as always, an

---

[132]Knolles, *Generall Historie of the Turkes*, p. 396.

[133]Knolles, *Generall Historie of the Turkes*, pp. 399-400; and Armstrong, *Heroes of Defeat*, p. 260.

Sultan Mehmed II

unreliable ally. The Albanians, led by Scanderbeg, once again found themselves in the position of having to rely mainly on their own resources to maintain their independence in face of Ottoman expansion, but these resources were steadily diminishing.

Mehmed II decided that the time had come to put an end to the obstinate Albanian resistance to Ottoman rule once and for all. In the summer of 1466, he personally led an army of nearly 100,000 men into Albania. The Ottomans met with stiff resistance as they fought their way through the rugged mountain passes into Albania. The Greek chronicler Kritovoulos informs us that: "There followed a great hand to hand battle, with attack and counter-attack, a terrible struggle, for the Illyrians [Albanians] resisted stoutly and fought bravely. But he [Mehmed] routed them and took the passes by force, and drove them out with great slaughter."[134]

Unable to stop the Ottomans from entering into the country, the Albanians retreated into the mountains; "the Illyrians [Albanians]," Kritovoulos recorded, "took their wives, flocks, and every other moveable up into the high and inaccessible mountain fortresses,"[135] employing a scorched-earth policy, following the same strategy they used in 1450. Albanian soldiers and peasants harassed the Ottoman army as it made its way toward Croya. Once

---

[134]Kritovoulos, *History of Mehmed the Conqueror*, p. 212 [V,66].

[135]Kritovoulos, *History of Mehmed the Conqueror*, p. 212 [V, 69].

again, Scanderbeg's heavily-fortified capital, defended by a small force of brave, resolute soldiers, withstood Ottoman artillery attacks, while he and his cavalry attacked the invaders from the rear. After two months, Mehmed withdrew half of his army from Croya, leaving the ever-present Ballaban Pasha, with the other half, to continue the siege, hoping to starve the fortress into submission.

The Sultan, meanwhile, proceeded southward where he constructed a fortress of his own, which he named Elbassan, with materials he had brought for this purpose.[136] That Mehmed had brought along materials to construct this fortress gives us some insight into his strategic thinking. He knew that the siege of Croya would distract the Albanians sufficiently to allow him time to construct this Ottoman stronghold in the very heart of Albania. From this outpost, Ottoman forces could wage war on the Albanian countryside and ravage the local economy. This is confirmed by Kritovoulos who reports: "[Mehmed planned to] leave a

---

[136]Sphrantzes, *The Fall of the Byzantine Empire*, p. 87 [XLIII.3]; and Kritovoulos, *History of Mehmed the Conqueror*, p. 211 [V,65]. The Ottoman chronicler Ashik Pashazade described the campaign as follows: "The Sultan, with great magnificence, set out for the vilayet of the Albanians. After he gathered an army he entered the vilayet of the Albanians and sent the cavalry and the soldiers he had brought with him all over the countryside. Some Albanian lords came to him, while others fled and disappeared. The Sultan also constructed a fortress in the middle of the vilayet of the Albanians. It was called Elbassan. He placed warriors in this fortress. They made raids upon the land all around it." In *Burime osmane*, pp. 70-71 [f. 169]. Similar accounts are provided by Oruç in *Burime osmane*, p. 47; and "Kronikat osmane anonime," in *Burime osmane*, pp. 55-56 [f. 70].

considerable army there which should constantly ravage
and plunder, and never allow the Illyrians to leave their city
or come down from the mountains during the winter to till
the land or to pasture or care for their flocks, or do anything
else. Thus, as they would be continuously so confined and
undergoing hardships, they would one day be compelled to
submit to the Sultan."[137]

After constructing Elbassan and installing an Ottoman
garrison there, Mehmed returned to Constantinople. Scanderbeg now had to deal with both Ballaban Pasha's siege of
Croya and the threat posed by the Turkish forces at Elbassan. During the fall of 1466, he tried to cut the Ottoman supply lines in an attempt to force them to lift the siege of
Croya. According to the Ottoman chronicler Tursun Beg,
the Albanians, "Under the leadership of Iskender [Scander-
beg], nicknamed Ha'in [the Traitor], planned to attack the
fortress at Elbassan."[138]

The Ottoman stronghold in central Albania represented
a threat not only to Scanderbeg, but also to the Venetians.
The danger prompted the Senate of the Republic of St. Mark
to adopt the following decision, on 16 August 1466, by a
vote of 94 to 2, with 6 abstentions: "All those who write from
Albania consider it to be a dangerous and harmful thing for
our possessions in Albania the rebuilding the Turks are doing of the city called Valmi [Elbassan], both because of its

---

[137]Kritovoulos, *History of Mehmed the Conqueror*, p. 214 [V,77].

[138]Tursun Beg, *The History of Mehmed the Conqueror*, p. 56 [124a].

proximity to our lands and because of the abundance of materials in the surrounding area to build barks and other
boats, as well as the ease with which they could descend
down the river from this location and into the sea. Therefore, as it is necessary to take all measures on every part, the
decision shall be adopted and written in the proper form
and sent to the magnificent lord Scanderbeg, asking that he
have the goodwill to address this plague that is to be found
in his and our very bosom, as the danger grows with every
passing day. Also, let it be written to our Governor in
Shkodra that, because of this situation, it is necessary that
he meet with the aforementioned Scanderbeg, to find out his
opinions, and to remind him that it would be very much to
our satisfaction, and that we would remain pleased, if he
would have the boldness (taking into consideration the position of the land and the number of the enemy, the task can,
perhaps, be accomplished with certainty) to gather all our
Venetian and Italian people, both infantry and cavalry, together with his own military forces (which all combined
should provide a large number of troops, superior to those
of the enemy) and assault that place [Elbassan], and, after
expelling the Turks, destroy it. At this time, we make the
decision that three thousand ducats, necessary for Albania,
be sent without delay by bark to our Governor in Albania,
so that, if the Lord Scanderbeg is willing to undertake this
expedition, it will be possible to reward those who take part
in it, Italians or others, as he sees fit. It is also necessary to
command that all of our aforementioned soldiers obey the

GEORGIVS CASTRIOTVS SCANDERBEGVS,
Epiri & Albaniæ &c. Princeps Anno 1 4 4 4.

Pellæus, Pyrrhusq̃, GEORGII in pectore, reges,
Thracem ex Epiro quando fugabat, erant.

T E, rex Epiri donauit pectore Pyrrhus,
    Nomine præterea rex Macedumq̃, suo:
Inciderat quanquam tua non in tempora virtus
Commoda, sic verpis Thracibus horror eras.
A Pyrrho, duce te, capta olim Roma, GEORGI,
    Orbis Alexandrum regem habiturus erat.

                 C   FRAN-

orders of the aforementioned Lord Scanderbeg and our Governor of Albania, and that they go in companionship, together with the aforementioned Scanderbeg, having the duty to secure all of our lands in Albania, and especially our city, Shkodra."[139]

These efforts also failed to yield any positive results as the siege of Croya continued. The situation in Albania became critical and defeat seemed imminent; rumors began to spread throughout Europe that Scanderbeg had at last been vanquished and that Albania had fallen to the Ottomans.[140] Determined to crush Scanderbeg, the Turkish forces led by Ballaban Pasha maintained the siege of Croya throughout the winter; something unusual for Ottoman armies that generally disbanded during the winter months. Realizing the desperation of situation, Scanderbeg set out for Italy in December, 1466, hoping to obtain foreign support to drive the invaders from his lands. The fact that he left Albania demonstrates two things. First of all, the seriousness of the situation, which he believed required him to go abroad to appeal personally for assistance. Up to this time, he had left Albania only when the situation was secure, now he did so even as the enemy besieged his capital. Secondly, it tells us that the Ottoman forces were ineffective during the winter

---

[139]Dok. 238, Vendim I Senatit të Venedikut në lidhje me ndërtimin e kalasë Valmi (Elbasan) nga turqit, 16 gusht 1466," in *Burime të zgjedhura*, vol.. II, pp. 346-347.

[140]Setton, *Papacy and the Levant*, vol. II, p. 278; and Pastor, *History of the Popes*, vol. IV, p. 86.

months and, although they could blockade the city, the well-provisioned garrison was in no immediate danger.

The Mantuan ambassador to the Vatican described the Albanian leader's arrival at the Holy See: "The lord Scanderbeg arrived here Friday [12 December 1466], and the households of the cardinals were sent out to meet him. He is a man of advanced age, past sixty; he has come with few horses, a poor man. I understand he will seek aid."[141] After spending a month in Rome, and receiving a welcome deserving of a living legend the he had become, Scanderbeg only managed to secure minimal support from the Pope who did not want to invest heavily in what appeared to him to be a lost cause. The Albanian leader left Rome with 5,000 ducats, and proceeded to Naples where he received weapons, supplies, and an additional 1,000 ducats from King Ferrante.[142]

Scanderbeg returned to Albania in early spring and prepared his counter-offensive. In April, 1467, he launched a fierce attack against the Ottoman attackers, who had been weakened by the harsh winter, and decisively defeated the besiegers. Writing from Venice, Zakaria Barbarus described

---

[141]Quoted in Setton, *Papacy and the Levant*, vol. II, p. 279; see also "Dok. 239, Nga letra e I.P. Arrivabenus mbi arritjen e Skenderbeut në Roma, 12 dhjetor 1466," in *Burime të zgjedhura*, vol. II, p. 349.

[142]"Dok. 240, Letër e Ferdinandit, mbreti I Napolit, drejtuar protonoterit Roka në Romë mbi vizitën e Skenderbeut në Napoli, 26 mars, 1467," in *Burime të zgjedhura*, vol. II p. 349.

the battle in a letter to the Bishop of Verona: "Today we received a letter dated 27 April from our Rector [Governor] in
Alessio who has learned that Scanderbeg, with 1,500 troops,
has captured the brother of Ballaban, the Sultan's General,
together with all the equipment that they [the Ottomans]
had used against Croya, and has brought them to Alessio.
Ballaban, suspecting that he could not come to the aid of his
forces in Croya, decided to assault the city and launched an
attack. Those inside conducted themselves bravely and
wounded the aforementioned Ballaban, General of the Sultan, with the first shot. As soon as he was brought back to
his camp he died. Scanderbeg then arrived and expelled all
of the Turks from their camp, taking control of Croya and
reinforcing it with weapons, he killed many of the Turks
and won a great victory... It is hoped that all those who had
risen up against Scanderbeg during the Turkish invasion
will return their allegiance to him."[143]

After relieving Croya, Scanderbeg could at last make
use of the promised Venetian support for an attack against
the newly constructed Ottoman citadel at Elbassan.[144] The
Turkish occupation of Elbassan, a navigable outlet to the
Adriatic Sea, situated on the Shkumbi river, presented a

---

[143]"Dok. 241, Letër e Zakaria Barabus në Venedik drejtuar peshkopit të
Veronës mbi fitoren e Skenderbeut kundër Ballaban Pashës, 10 maj
1467," in *Burime të zgjedhura*, vol. II, p. 350.

[144]"Dok. 238, Vendim I Senatit të Venedikut në lidhje me ndërtimin e
kalasë Valmi (Elbasan) nga turqit," in *Burime të zgjedhura*, vol. II, pp. 346-
347; and Kritovoulos, *History of Mehmed the Conqueror*, p. 218 [V,91].

clear threat to Venetian interests in Albania. The joint Albanian-Venetian siege failed, however, because the citadel was strongly fortified, and it had to be abandoned when Mehmed II led a new expedition into Albania. Kritoboulos informs us that the Sultan invaded Albania in a rage after Ballaban Pasha's defeat: "He also pursued their prince, Alexander [Scanderbeg], who took refuge in the inaccessible fortresses of the mountains, in his customary retreats and abodes in the hills."[145]

An Ottoman army as large as that of the previous year entered Albania in July, 1467, and again laid siege to Scanderbeg's capital. After only three weeks Mehmed had to withdrew the main body of his army from the country, leaving only a small contingent to continue the siege of Croya.[146] The outbreak of plague, which struck the Balkans and Asia Minor during the summer of 1467, may have hastened the Sultan's departure. Shortly after Mehmed withdrew, Scanderbeg defeated the remaining Ottoman forces and again lifted the siege of Croya.[147]

By the fall of 1467 he had regained control over his territories; only Elbassan remained in Ottoman hands. Mehmed's determined efforts had met with failure. Albania had proved to be a costly battleground for the Ottomans,

---

[145]Kritovoulos, *History of Mehmed the Conqueror*, p. 218 [V,91].

[146]Kritovoulos, *History of Mehmed the Conqueror*, p. 219 [V,99].

[147]"Dok. 243, Nga një kronikë venedikase mbi rrethimin e tretë të Krujës," in *Burime të zgjedhura*, vol. II, p. 351.

but its inhabitants also paid a high price for their resistance. The economy was devastated. Large numbers of Albanians had been killed in battle during the Ottoman invasions, while others had fled to southern Italy. Despite this, the Albanians, using every resource at their disposal, continued their struggle to maintain their independence from the Islamic Empire.

Chapter VI
The Fall of Albania to the Ottoman Turks

"Though his lands were ravaged, the courage of Castriot was not wearied, nor was his genius baffled, until, in the year 1468, there came upon him a mightier than Ballaban, or a mightier than Mahomet."

— James Ludlow, *The Captain of the Janizaries*[148]

After repulsing the Ottoman invaders in the summer of 1467, Scanderbeg was determined to oust the Sultan's garrison from Elbassan. To this end, in January, 1468, he went to Alessio to seek support from the Venetians, who continued their war against the Turks, in hopes of organizing a joint assault on the fortress.[149] Tragedy struck for the Albanians when, while in Alessio, Scanderbeg contracted a malignant

---

[148]Ludlow, *The Captain of the Janizaries*, p. 404.

[149]Knolles, *Generall Historie of the Turkes*, p. 402.

fever, probably a result of the plague, and, after a brief illness, he died on 17 January 1468.[150]

Realizing that Albania could no longer resist the Ottomans without foreign support, Scanderbeg bequeathed his lands to the Republic of St. Mark[151] until his son John was old enough to take possession of them. The Albanian leader was buried in the Church of St. Nicholas[152] where the League of Alessio had been founded in 1444.

Scanderbeg's death dealt a severe blow to the Albanian resistance. His leadership, political skill, and military genius had been essential elements in the Albanian success. With their leader dead and resources becoming scarcer with each passing year, the Albanian cause appeared doomed. Upon hearing of Scanderbeg's death, Mehmed the Conqueror is said to have declared, "At last Europe and Asia are mine. Woe to Christendom! She has lost her sword and shield!"[153]

---

[150]"Dok. 244, Nga letra që Gerardus de Kolis në Venedik I dërgon Dukës së Milanos Galeaco Sforcas, 12 shkurt 1468; Dok. 246, Ngushëllimet e Ferdinandit, mbretit të Napolit drejtuar Donikës, së vejës së Skenderbeut, 24 shkurt 1468; and Dok. 247, Letër e mbretit Ferdinand drejtuar Jeronim de Karvinjo, 24 shkurt 1468," in Burime të zgjedhura, vol. II, pp. 353-355; Setton, *Papacy and the Levant*, vol. II, p. 290; and Pastor, *History of the Popes*, vol. IV, p. 90

[151]"Dok. 245, Vendim I Senatit të Venedikut mbi masat në Shqipëri pas vdekes së Skenderbeut, 13 shkurt 1468," in *Burime të zgjedhura*, vol. II, pp. 351-354.

[152]Knolles, *Generall Historie of the Turkes*, pp. 402-403.

[153]quoted in Pastor, *History of the Popes*, vol. IV, p. 90.

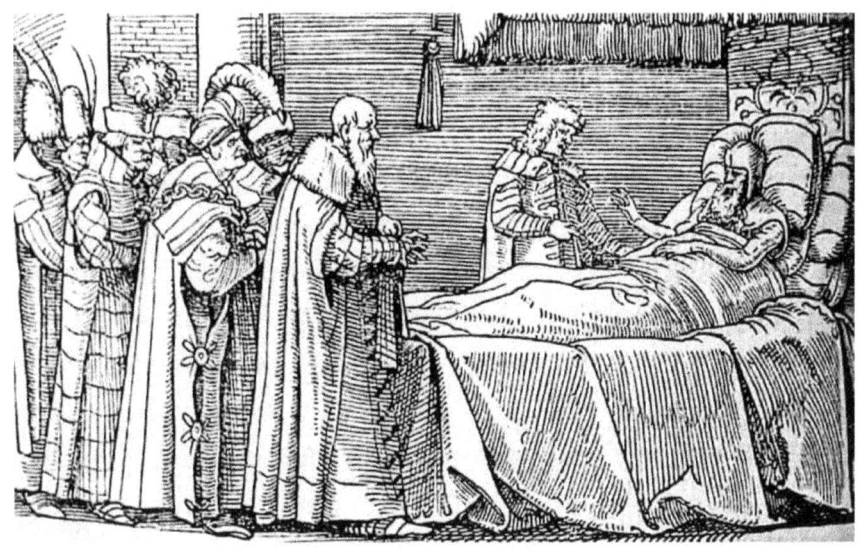

Death of Scanderbeg, January 17, 1468

The steady depopulation of the country also weakened the Albanian resistance. The wars took countless lives, and the massive invasions led by Mehmed II in 1466 and 1467 sparked a large-scale emigration to southern Italy and Venice, which increased after Scanderbeg's death and continued until the end of the century. Apart from the disruption of everyday life brought about by the constant wars, a major reason for this emigration to Italy was that the devastated economy could no longer support the population. By the end of the century, as many as 200,000 Albanians had fled to Italy, depopulating entire villages.[154] Among those who left for Italy after Scanderbeg's death were his wife and his young son John, who settled on the estates which King Ferrante of Naples had granted to Scanderbeg after his expedition in Italy. Three centuries later, British traveler Henry Swinburne could still see evidence of this migration: "The death of Scanderbeg removed every obstacle to the Turkish conquests, and his son John fled to Naples for refuge. He was received with open arms, lands were assigned to his followers, and exemption from taxes granted them, with many other privileges, of which some shadow still remains."[155]

---

[154]Pulaha, "Aspectes de demographie historique," p. 65; Pulaha, *On the Demographic and Ethnical Situation of the Albanian Territories (15th-16th Centuries)*; and Fine, *Late Medieval Balkans*, p. 611.

[155]Swinburne, *Travels in the Two Sicilies*, vol. I, p. 350. See also Knolles, *Generall Historie of the Turkes*, p. 402.

Despite the death of their leader, the Albanians, with Venetian assistance, continued to resist Ottoman domination. As the war with Venice raged on, it was almost ten years before the Sultan again turned his attention to Albania; in 1477, Mehmed the Conqueror initiated the final siege of Scanderbeg's mighty capital, Croya. A contemporary of these events, the Ottoman chronicler Tursun Beg, described the Sultan's strategy: "Sultan Mehmed first of all took control over all the sea and land routes by which supplies or reinforcements could reach the fortress and planned to starve it into submission."[156]

While besieging Croya, Ottoman forces, applying the same strategy, also laid siege to Shkodra,[157] the most important of the Venetian possessions in Albania. Starved into submission, the fortress of Croya, which had previously survived three major sieges under the leadership of Scanderbeg, finally surrendered to the Ottomans in June, 1478.

Venice, realizing that it could not benefit from a continuation of hostilities, resolved to make peace with the Sultan. The events in Albania, combined with the death of the Turkoman ruler Uzun Hasan, early in 1468, upon whom the Venetians had relied to force Mehmed to commit resources to

---

[156]Tursun Beg, *History of Mehmed the Conqueror*, p. 63.

[157]An eyewitness account of the seige of Shkodra is provided by the Albanian chronicler and cleric Marin Barletti. See Barleci, *Rrethimi i Shkodres*.

eastern Anatolia,[158] influenced their decision to seek peace. The Ottomans and Venice concluded a peace treaty, on 25 January 1479, when the Venetian commissioner Giovanni Dario signed the document in Istanbul. By the terms of the treaty, the Venetians surrendered most of Albania to the Sultan, including Shkodra, which was still under siege at the time. In return, Venice preserved its trading privileges in the Levant, agreeing to pay 10,000 ducats annually for these rights in addition to the 100,000 gold ducats owed by the Venetian lessees of some Turkish alum mines.[159]

For all intents and purposes the Albanian resistance to the Ottomans appeared to be at an end. The peace treaty ending the Ottoman-Venetian war which had begun in 1463 not only brought an end to the rebellion begun by Scander-beg in 1443, but it also made Albania a potential base for Ottoman expansion into Italy which was then beset by its own internal difficulties.

---

[158]Setton, *Papacy and the Levant,* vol. II, p. 321.

[159]Setton, *Papacy and the Levant,* vol. II, pp. 327-328 for details of the treaty; and Pastor, *History of the Popes,* vol. IV, p. 332.

Chapter VII
The Ottoman Invasion of Italy
and the Albanian Rebellion, 1480-1481

"In Rome, the alarm was as great as if the enemy
had been already encamped before her very
walls.... Terror had taken such hold of all minds
that even the Pope meditated flight."

— Sigismondo de'Conti[160]

The fall of Albania had opened the doors to Italy and, in
1480, the Ottoman army crossed the Adriatic Sea, from its
port at Vlora on the Albanian coast, and landed on the
shores of Puglia in the Kingdom of Naples, capturing Otranto. Panic spread throughout Italy, as reflected in the report of the papal secretary Sigismondo de'Conti. King Ferrante of Naples recalled his son Alphonso, the Duke of Calabria, with the Neapolitan army from Tuscany to meet the
threat, while at the same time he appealed for assistance
from the Christian powers of Europe.[161]

---

[160]quoted in Pastor, *History of the Popes*, vol. IV, p. 334.

[161]Cambini, *Two Commentaries*, pp. 35-36.

SIXTVS·IIII·PONT·MAX·CREA·ANN·1471

Pope Sixtus IV

It seemed as if Sultan Mehmed II, the conqueror of Constantinople, was now on his way to Rome. According to the Venetian Niccolo Sagundino, Mehmed believed that Constantinople was the daughter of Rome, and now that he had the daughter, he also wanted to have the mother.[162] Despite the dramatic entry of the Ottomans into Italy, within little more than a year the danger had subsided; Otranto was recaptured by the Neapolitan forces and the mighty conqueror who had made Europe tremble for thirty years was dead.

On the eve of the Ottoman invasion, Italy was divided against itself. Few had noticed as the last remnants as Scanderbeg's resistance in Albania succumbed to Turkish domination, and even fewer realized the imminent danger that this posed to Italy. Pope Sixtus IV's practice of nepotism and his attempts to expand papal influence aggravated the dissension among the Italian states. On 26 April 1478, rival Florentine patriciate families, assisted by Sixtus IV's nephew Girolamo Riaro, attempted to kill Guliano and Lorenzo de'Medici and seize power in Florence. The Piazza Conspiracy, as the event is known, failed. The conspirators killed Guliano de'Medici, but only wounded Lorenzo, who escaped and emerged from the affair in firmer control of Florence than ever before.

This incident renewed warfare among the Italian states. Venice, Milan, and Ferrara joined Florence against the Pope,

---

[162]Babinger, *Mehmed the Conqueror*, p. 495.

while Ferrante, the King of Naples, joined the papal side in hopes of acquiring Siena.[163] Ferrante sent his son Alphonso, the Duke of Calabria, with the Neapolitan army to Tuscany where he defeated the Florentines. Faced with this threat, Lorenzo de'Medici traveled to Naples to negotiate with Ferrante. A peace treaty concluded between Naples and Florence in March, 1480, resulted in an agreement between the two states to cooperate in their efforts to limit papal and Venetian expansion. This change of alliances strained relations between Ferrante and the Pope, who now turned to Venice for support against Naples. On the eve of the invasion, Italy was thus in turmoil, a circumstance of which the Ottomans took full advantage.

The Ottoman plan to invade southern Italy was well conceived. In the summer of 1479, Mehmed II appointed Ahmed Gedik Pasha as sandjakbey of Vlora to prepare for an invasion of the Kingdom of Naples. One of the Sultan's ablest commanders, Ahmed Gedik Pasha had become Grand Vizier in 1474; the following year he led the forces that captured the Crimean city of Caffa from the Genoese.[164] He later fell out of favor with the Sultan and was imprisoned when he disagreed with the plan to besiege Shkodra.

---

[163]Setton, *Papacy and the Levant*, vol. II, pp. 336-338.

[164]For details of Ahmed Gedik Pasha's career see Inalcik, "Ahmed Gedik Pasha," in *Encyclopedia of Islam*, vol. I, pp. 292-293.

He was soon released and appointed sandjakbey of Salonika, before being sent to Vlora to begin preparing for the Otranto expedition.[165]

There were three stages to Ahmed Gedik Pasha's preparations; the first being to strengthen Ottoman control over southern Albania. The Venetian chronicler Stefano Magno informs us that shortly after his arrival in Vlora, Ahmed Gedik Pasha campaigned all along the coast of southern Albania, fortifying strategic positions and taking possession of the fortresses of Himara and Sopot from the Venetians in accordance with the peace treaty which ended the Ottoman-Venetian conflict.[166]

These acquisitions were a necessary prerequisite to launching an invasion of Italy because the invasion force would depend upon supplies and reinforcements, as well as communications, from southern Albania. The second part of the Ottomans preparations involved seizing the islands of Santa Maura and Zante, then held by Ferrante's ally Leo-

---

[165]Ottoman sources make it clear that Ahmed Gedik Pasha was sent to Vlora specifically to prepre for the Italian expedition. See Hoxha Sadeddin, "Tacut-tevarih" in *Burime osmane*, pp. 268-269; and Sollakzade [Mehmet Hemdimi], "Tarih-I Solakzade," in *Burime osmane*, p. 307.

[166]"Dok. 45, Nga Drsh. i Stefano Magnos," in *Dokumenta të shekullit XV*, vol. IV, pt. 1, p. 47; "Dok. 251, Pjesë nga kronika e Stefano Manjos," in *Burime të zgjedhura*, vol. II, p. 359; and Stefano Magno, "Evenements historique en Grece (1479-1497)," in *Documents inedits relatifs a l'histoire de la Grece au Moyen Age*, t. 6, p. 218.

nardo Tocco. On 26 August 1479, Leonardi Bottae, the Milanese representative in Venice, reported that the Ottoman fleet was en route to Santa Maura: "The Signoria has told me that, with the letter from their rectorate in Corfu, there has come news that the whole fleet which was in Vlora has passed through the channel of Corfu and, without stopping anywhere, has gone in the direction of Santa Maura."[167]

By the first of September, Santa Maura and Zante had been captured, but the mission also exposed the continued vulnerability of the Ottoman positions along the Albanian coast. Leonardi Bottae reported that, while the Ottoman fleet was operating in the Adriatic, pirates raided their principal port: "in Vlora 8 small barks stopped, which had passed through this gulf, gaining something..., but they were unable to cause great damage."[168]

With the seizure of Santa Maura and Zante Ahmed Gedik Pasha had secured safe passage across the Adriatic because the peace treaty with Venice had already neutralized their fleet at Corfu. While continuing to strengthen the Ottoman grip on Albania, he began gathering his invasion

---

[167]"Dok. 36, Perfaqesuesi milanez në Venedik [Leonardi Bottae] informon se flota turke e Vlorës ka kaluar nepër kanalin e Korfuzit, 26 gusht 1479," in *Dokumenta të shekullit XV*, vol. IV, pt. 1, p. 43.

[168]"Dok. 38, Perfaqesuesi i Milanos në Venedik [Leonardi Bottae] informon rreth veprimeve to flotës turke në Leukade dhe per fustet e Vlorës qe kane dalur në detin Adriatik, 1 shtator 1479," in *Dokumenta të shekullit XV*, vol. IV, pt. 1, p. 44.

force at Vlora. This was the logical base for Ottoman expansion into Italy. In addition to being the best Ottoman seaport on the eastern shore of the Adriatic, Vlora was located less than fifty miles from Puglia, making it the shortest sea route from Ottoman controlled territory to the Italian mainland. Even in ancient times, Greek sailors traveling to Italy would sail up the coast of the Adriatic to Epirus and cross the straits of Otranto.

Given the logistical problems of communications and of transporting troops and supplies, as well as the strategic difficulties of this type of military operation, the shortest sea route was most desirable. The galley was not a naval vessel designed to stay out at sea for long periods of time. As John Guilmartin has pointed out: "Tied strategically to its bases by the need for frequent revictualing and to the land by the need to take on water at even more frequent intervals, the galley fleet was tied even more closely to the shoreline by tactical considerations.... The logistical burden imposed by its large crew and its narrow hull with small internal capacity forced the galley to touch shore frequently."[169]

An additional reason to keep the nautical distance to a minimum was that communications between Italy and Istanbul were quickest by land. For example, Venice would typically send its communications to the Ottoman capital by

---

[169]Guilmartin, *Gunpowder and Galleys,* p. 57.

ship to Cattaro and then from there by land to Istanbul via Adrianople.[170]

Though a force to be reckoned with, the Ottoman navy was not yet the dominant naval power in the eastern Mediterranean that it would become in the next century. Since the transport of troops and supplies was crucial to the success of the invasion, the Ottoman desire to keep the distance as short as possible made perfect sense.

The Neapolitans were not ignorant of the Ottoman preparations in Albania. Leonardi Bottae informs us that already in mid-August, 1479 there was concern in Naples and along the eastern coast of Italy about the Turkish military build-up at Vlora: "Here it is heard that the Sultan's fleet, which is situated in Vlora, is now going out to enter this bay [of the Adriatic] and that, among the materials and other instruments of war which they bring with them, the Signoria is notified that they also bring with them three large bombards, the size of which is unmatched in Italy. All the shores of Marcha, Apruzo, and Puglia are in a great state of fear from this, because it is not known where the said fleet was headed. And, though here it is maintained as a thing of certainty that King Ferdinand is in agreement with the Sultan, nevertheless, with the letters that come from Naples, it is

---

[170]Treptow, "Distance and Communications in Southeastern Europe," pp. 475-476. See also Ranke, *Sämmliche Werke*, vol. 44, p. 526.

understood that His Majesty, from fear of the said fleet, has sent 300 soldiers to Brindiz."[171]

Although Ferrante was well aware of the Turkish activities at Vlora, the Neapolitan king did little to fortify his coastal defenses. The Neapolitans may have believed that Santa Maura and Zante were the ultimate Ottoman military objectives. Certainly, given the tense situation in Italy resulting from the Tuscan war, Ferrante would have liked to believe this to be the case; such optimism was, however, unwarranted. On 9 January 1480, the rector of Ragusa informed the Neapolitan king that the Turkish military build-up at Vlora was continuing throughout the winter: "Near Apollonia [Vlora] the preparations of the infantry and cavalry armies of the Turks which have gathered there appear to be very great; they have brought a multitude of ammunition that is used for war and with insistence the fleet is being strengthened; through the various roads from Constantinople as well as from other places is being expected not a small fleet."[172]

Preoccupied with Italian affairs, and perhaps not fully aware of the bold nature of Ahmed Gedik Pasha's plans,

---

[171]"Dok. 34, Pjese nga letra e perfaqesuesit te Milanos në Venedik [Leonardi Bottae], 14 gusht 1479," in *Dokumenta të shekullit XV*, vol. IV, pt. 1, p. 42.

[172]"Dok. 48, Rektori i keshillit te Raguzës i shkruan mbretit te Napolit mbi pregatitjet e turqve prane Vlorës, 9 janar 1480," in *Dokumenta të shekullit XV*, vol. IV, pt. 1, p. 49

King Ferrante of Naples

Ferrante continued to neglect his coastal defenses. Therefore, when the Ottomans invaded Italy, despite these advanced warnings, the Neapolitans were caught unprepared.

The invasion of Italy was only one part of the grandiose plans of Mehmed the Conqueror in 1480. In May of that year Ottoman forces besieged the island of Rhodes off the southwestern coast of Anatolia. The island was ably defended by the knights of St. John, led by Pierre d'Aubusson, who, with assistance received from the Pope and several of the Christian powers of Europe, staunchly resisted the Turkish assaults. Attacks on the well-fortified positions of the knights failed, and the Sultan's army finally had to abandon the siege in August, 1480.[173] This siege may have diverted Ferrante's attention away from his coastal defenses because the Neapolitans, perhaps, doubted the Ottomans would attempt such a major expedition as the invasion of Italy while it was in progress.

While Pope Sixtus IV tried to rally support for the Knights of St. John, a second disaster befell Christendom. The Ottoman chronicler Tursun Beg reported that Mehmed the Conqueror: "sent Gedik Ahmed Pasha with a large fleet to Pulya [Puglia] where he captured the fortress and converted the churches into mosques."[174]

---

[173]For a detailed study of the seige of Rhodes, see Brockman, *The Two Seiges of Rhodes, 1480-1522.*

[174]Tursun Beg, *History of Mehmed the Conqueror*, p. 63.

According to the Venetian chronicler Domenico Malipiero: "The Turks embarked from Vlora with 70 ships, and went in the direction of Otranto. And the [Venetian] general embarked [from Corfu] with 60 ships and followed them, holding them always in sight."[175] In subsequent accounts the total number of Ottoman ships has been exaggerated to as many as 140,[176] but there is little reason to doubt Malipiero's account because his sources were excellent and he was a contemporary of these events.

Likewise, the number of soldiers that Ahmed Gedik Pasha led ashore in southern Italy is also disputed. Estimates range from slightly less than 10,000 to as high as 18,000.[177] Given that the Ottoman galleys carried approximately 150 oarsmen and as many as 250 additional troops,[178] and that an unknown portion of the 70 ships were not galleys, but transport vessels used mainly to carry horses, cannon, am-

---

[175]"Dok. 64, Nga Vjetoret e D. Malipieros," in *Dokumenta të shekullit XV*, vol. IV, pt. 1, p. 59.

[176]Sismonde, *Histoire des républiques italiennes*, t. VII, p. 177, claims 100 ships. Babinger, *Mehmed the Conqueror*, p. 390 and Bentley, *Politics and Culture*, p. 129, both claim 140.

[177]Islami and Frashëri, *Historia e popullit shqiptar*, vol. I, p. 293, and Setton, *Papacy and the Levant*, vol. II, p. 344, both hold that Ahmed Gedik Pasha had 10,000 troops. Bentley, *Politics and Culture*, p. 29, Babinger, *Mehmed the Conqueror*, p. 390, and Schwoebel, *The Shadow of the Crescent*, p. 171, all claim an Ottoman invasion force of 18,000 men.

[178]Parker, *The Military Revolution*, p. 89.

munition, and other supplies and equipment, it is not unreasonable to assume a minimum landing force of 12,500 soldiers (an average of 250 troops aboard each of 50 vessels). Of course, this figure would be higher if the oarsmen were taken ashore as soldiers and the galleys towed back across the Adriatic to Vlora. There is some evidence to suggest that this is indeed what happened.

The German historian Franz Babinger claimed outright that the Venetians assisted the Ottomans by towing their galleys.[179] A contemporary, the Florentine bookseller Vespasiano da Bisticci reported that the Venetians: "remained neutral or even gave secret help to the enemy... all along there was a constant intercourse of their ships with the Turkish fleet."[180] Malipiero's reference that the Venetian fleet closely followed the Ottomans across the straits of Otranto and did not return to Corfu for 26 days[181] supports Vespasiano's account. Though it is unlikely that they would carry military supplies, the possibility that the Venetians also transported provisions for this invasion force should not be ruled out in light of this evidence and their collaboration with Murad II during his siege of Croya in 1450. From these facts, it can be inferred that the Ottoman landing force consisted of at least 12,500 to as many as 18,000 men. This

---

[179]Babinger, *Mehmed the Conqueror*, p. 395.

[180]Vespasiano da Bisticci, *Renaissance Princes, Popes, and Prelates*, p. 151.

[181]"Dok. 64, Nga Vjetoret e D. Malipieros," in *Dokumenta të shekullit XV*, vol. IV, pt. 1, p. 59.

army had been brought overland to Vlora in early June, 1480.

The Ottoman invasion force landed on the shores of Puglia, in the Kingdom of Naples, on 28 July 1480. After sending out an advance force to conduct reconnaissance and pillage the countryside, Ahmed Gedik Pasha disembarked the main body of his troops and laid siege to the city of Otranto. This had been the Pasha's intention all along, provided that the landing could be effected without serious opposition; he had brought artillery and siege machinery for this very purpose.[182]

The Italians at Otranto were caught by surprise. The city tried to hold out in hopes that Ferrante could send relief, but it was to no avail. On 11 August 1480, the Ottomans launched an assault and captured the city.[183] Mehmed the Conqueror now had a foothold on Italian soil from which he could strike out at his arch-enemies, Ferrante and the Pope.

Though Otranto was devastated and a number of people were killed or sent aboard Ottoman ships to Greece where they were sold into slavery, the Ottomans were restrained in their use of terror. They hoped to garner support from the local population against Ferrante who had never

---

[182]Cambini, *Two Commentaries*, p. 35; Simonde de Sismonde, *Histoire des républiques italiennes*, t. VII, p. 177; and Knolles, *Generall Historie of the Turkes*, p. 432.

[183]Cambini, *Two Commentaries*, p. 35; and Simonde de Sismondi, *Histoire des républiques italiennes*, t. VII, p. 177.

The Ottoman Invasion of Italy

been especially popular in this region. It should be remembered that the Prince of Taranto had been one of the leaders of the Angevin opposition to the installation of Ferrante as King of Naples less than twenty years earlier.

When the Ottomans landed in Puglia the main part of Ferrante's army, under the command of his son Alfonso, the Duke of Calabria, was still stationed in Tuscany, despite the peace treaty concluded with the Florentines earlier in the year. On 2 August 1480, Ferrante wrote to Alfonso, ordering him to come to the defense of Otranto, which was then under siege by the Ottomans. Unfortunately for the Neapolitans, Alfonso did not reach Otranto until 10 September, long after the city had fallen to the Turks. In desperation, Ferrante issued an appeal for assistance to the Pope and the Christian powers of Europe.[184]

The relationship between Ferrante and the Pope had steadily deteriorated since Naples had made peace with Florence in the spring of 1480. The papal secretary, Sigismondo de'Conti, wrote: "Sixtus IV would have witnessed with great indifference the misfortunes and losses of his faithless ally had Ferrante's enemy had been anyone but the Sultan; but it was a very different matter when the common foe of Christendom had actually got footing on Italian soil."[185] Ferrante commissioned Giovanni de'Margheriti,

---

[184]Cambini, *Two Commentaries*, p. 35-36.

[185]quoted in Pastor, *History of the Popes*, vol. IV, p. 335.

the bishop of Girona, to solicit assistance from Sixtus IV. According to Malipiero, Ferrante relayed the message to the Pope that if he did not receive assistance, "he would allow the passage of the Turkish army through the Kingdom of Naples to go to Rome."[186]

Though initially Sixtus IV contemplated fleeing to Avignon, his position as leader of all Christendom bound him to assist Ferrante in his efforts to expel the Turks from Italy. After meeting with the Pope, the bishop of Girona proceeded to Venice. Ferrante hoped that the Italian states would lend him assistance, and Venetian support would be the key to the formation of any united Italian resistance against the Ottoman invaders. Margheriti's mission to "exhort the Venetians, as the greatest sea power, that it might please them to lend their aid in time of danger to King Ferdinand...," proved in vain, Vespasiano writes, because "the Venetians were not to be moved."[187]

Venice and Naples had long been rivals for power and influence in Italy, as well as in Albania. After a long, disastrous war with the Ottomans, the Venetians wanted to

---

[186]"Dok. 64, Nga Vjetoret e D. Malipieros," in *Dokumenta të shekullit XV*, vol. IV, pt. 1, p. 59.

[187]Vespasiano da Bisticci, *Renaissance Princes, Popes, and Prelates*, p. 151.

maintain peaceful relations with the Porte at all costs.[188]
Their prosperity depended upon their Levant trade and further hostilities with the Turks at this time could only damage that. Venetian officials knew of Ahmed Gedik Pasha's
invasion plan six months to a year before the attack on Otranto[189] and did nothing to impede its execution. Clearly,
Venetian interests lay in avoiding conflict with the Sultan.
Given the mutual hostility between Venice and Naples,
Ludwig Pastor is probably correct in his assessment that, "If
the Signoria did not actually invite the Turks into Italy, they

---

[188]The role of Venice is one of the most controversial topics surrounding
the invasion of Otranto. Some, like J. Hammer and Le Comte Daru, have
argued that the Venetians actually persuaded the Sultan to undertake
the invasion in the first place, see Hammer, Histoire de l'empire
ottoman, vol. III, p. 260; and Le Comte Daru, Histoire de Venise, vol. I,
p. 270. Others have argued that Venice helped finance the invasion, see
Gegaj, L'Albanie et l'invasion turque, p. 154. Certainly the Venetians
knew of the invasion plan well in advance, but the Sultan certainly did
not need Venetian persuasion to launch the attack on his old enemy,
Ferrante. Kenneth Setton correctly pointed out that the invasion placed
the Republic of St. Mark in a difficult situation; on the one hand, it
desired to contain Neapolitan expansionism in Italy, it certainly did not
cherish the tought that the Ottomans would be left in control of both
coasts of the Adriatic which could potentially bottle up Venetian trade,
the life blood of the Republic. At the same time, it wanted to maintain
peaceful relations with the Sultan. Thus, the final outcome of the
Ottranto campaign was probably the best result that Venice could have
hoped for. See Setton, *Papacy and the Levant*, vol. II, p. 340, nt. 83. Though
they did not take part directly in the campaign, Venetian interests may
have compelled them to lend some assistance to the Ottomans.

[189]"Dok. 37, Pjesë e një kronikë venedike, gusht 1479," in *Dokumenta të
shekullit XV*, vol. IV, pt. 1, p. 44, which indicates that the Venetian Senate
received an envoy from Ahmed Gedik Pasha in August, 1479.

certainly allowed them to believe that their arrival would be far from unwelcome to them."[190]

At Rome, a Consistory decided that every possible effort should be made to assist Ferrante in expelling the Ottoman invaders from the Italian mainland,[191] but material aid was not forthcoming soon. The Neapolitans had to rely principally upon their own resources. After his recall from Tuscany, Alfonso recruited additional troops as he marched towards Puglia, but still his army consisted of a mere 3,000 men.[192]

Being seriously outnumbered by the invaders, Alfonso's forces could offer only token opposition. As they lacked the resources to lay siege to the city, the Neapolitans established their camp at a safe distance from Otranto; their purpose being to prevent further Ottoman conquests until additional men and materials would arrive. According to the Florentine writer Andrea Cambini, "there was daily skirmish between them of the camp and them of the town, but they of the camp had always the worse."[193]

After capturing Otranto, the Turks made raids on Lecce, Brindisi, and Taranto. These were punitive expeditions,

---

[190]Pastor, *History of the Popes*, vol. IV, p. 333.

[191]Pastor, *History of the Popes*, vol. IV, p. 336.

[192]Cambini, *Two Commentaries*, p. 35; and Armstrong, "The Papacy and Naples in the Fifteenth Century," *The Cambridge Medieval History, Volume 8: The Close of the Middle Ages*, p. 195.

[193]Cambini, *Two Commentaries*, p. 36.

aimed at frightening the Christians and procuring booty, rather than attempts to capture these cities. With the winter rapidly approaching, the Ottomans were more interested in consolidating their conquests than extending them. Ahmed Gedik Pasha concentrated on fortifying Otranto as a base for future expansion in Italy.[194] Having strengthened the city's defenses, the Turkish commander left a well-provisioned garrison of 8,000 troops in Otranto and returned to Vlora with the remainder of his forces to prepare for a spring expedition to extend Ottoman conquests in Italy.

Meanwhile, the Ottoman garrison in Italy, commanded by Hayreddin Bey, a Greek who spoke Italian, sought to garner support from the native population. The Sultan approved plans to offer a ten-year tax exemption and promised freedom of worship to those who cooperated with the invaders,[195] while those who resisted and fell captive were taken to Greece and sold into slavery. During the winter months neither side undertook significant military activities. The Neapolitans used the winter respite to garrison neighboring towns, while the Ottoman fleet raided the coast of Puglia and continued provisioning Otranto for the upcoming campaigning season.[196]

---

[194]Cambini, *Two Commentaries*, p. 36; Knolles, *Generall Historie of the Turkes*, p. 432; and Babinger, *Mehmed the Conqueror*, pp. 391-392.

[195]Simonde de Sismondi, *Histoire des républiques italiennes*, t. VII, p. 179; and Babinger, *Mehmed the Conqueror*, pp. 391-392.

[196]Cambini, *Two Commentaries*, p. 36.

Efforts by Ferrante and Sixtus IV to organize a counter-offensive against the Ottomans continued throughout the winter. On 15 December 1480, a Consistory agreed to contribute 150,000 ducats toward Christian efforts to relieve Otranto; 100,000 of these were to be used to equip and man a fleet of 25 galleys, while the other 50,000 ducats were sent to Matthias Corvinus with the intention that he organize an attack on the Ottomans from Hungary. In addition, 3,000 additional troops were sent to join the Christian forces already at Otranto.[197]

Sixtus IV hoped to use the Otranto crisis to organize a new crusade against the Turkish Infidels, but his appeals were received with little enthusiasm by the Christian powers of Europe. Despite the dim outlook for support, the Pope issued a plea for a crusade on 8 April 1481.[198] As a further inducement, on 20 April 1481, Sixtus offered indulgences to anyone who would join the war against the Ottomans.[199]

---

[197]Setton, *Papacy and the Levant*, vol. II, p. 368; and Pastor, *History of the Popes*, vol. IV, p. 337. As on other occasions, when the King of Hungary received money from the Pope for such a purpose, the plan for Matthias Corvinus to attack the Turks from Hungary never materialized. The idea was that such an attack would draw Ottoman resources away from Italy.

[198]"Dok. 70, Enciklikë e papës Sikstit të IV-te për kryqezate, 8 prill 1481," in *Dokumenta të shekullit XV*, vol. IV, pt. 1, p. 66.

[199]"Dok. 71, Ndjesë për ata qe do të ndihmojne për shpenzimet e luftës kundër turqve, 20 prill 1481," in *Dokumenta të shekullit XV*, vol. IV, pt. 1, p. 66.

Nevertheless, united European action against the Ottomans remained a dream that would not be realized. The Christian states of Europe were divided against themselves. This meant that Ferrante would have to rely mainly upon his own resources, with some aid from his Italian allies, namely Florence and Milan, as well as the Papacy. Having failed to secure a great deal of foreign assistance, Ferrante and Sixtus were certainly in peril at the prospect of a renewed Ottoman assault in the spring of 1481.

Across the Adriatic, the Ottomans faced a far greater danger to the continuation of their Italian campaign than the threat posed by the Neapolitan forces in Puglia. Shortly after the Turks invaded the Kingdom of Naples, a series of rebellions broke out in Albania. Though small and localized, these uprisings, if they intensified, could seriously threaten the Ottoman position in Italy by cutting off the communication and supply lines between Istanbul and Vlora. Securing control of Albania had been a necessary prerequisite to the invasion of Italy; now, revolts in Albania threatened to disrupt the expansion plans of Mehmed II and Ahmed Gedik Pasha.

The causes of the Albanian rebellion go back to the time of Scanderbeg. As the departure of a large portion of Ahmed Gedik Pasha's troops to Italy had weakened the Sultan's grip on the country, only recently secured, Albanians took advantage of the situation to try and free themselves once again from Turkish domination. They continued Scanderbeg's rebellion despite the fact that fifty years of organized resistance had seriously depleted the manpower and resources of the land. The independent spirit of the mountain people, combined with the legacy of the long resistance led by Scanderbeg, continued to foster rebellion in Albania.

After a winter respite, the Albanian rebellions increased in number and intensity. A contemporary of these events, the Venetian chronicler Stefano Magno, informs us that in February, 1481 the rebels attacked Ottoman and Venetian positions in Albania.[200] Meanwhile, Ahmed Gedik Pasha continued his preparations for the spring campaign in Italy. He gathered an army of 25,000 men that would cross the Adriatic to extend Ottoman conquests in Italy. Despite the presence of this sizeable force, the Turkish commander was aware that the Ottoman position in Albania remained tenuous. The Ottoman chronicler Ashik Pashazade tells us that the Albanian rebels defeated a force sent against them by Ahmed Gedik Pasha and captured their weapons and supplies.[201] This victory strengthened the Albanian resistance and delayed the departure of the Ottoman troops for Italy.

Then, on 3 May 1481, Mehmed II died while en route to a war against either Rhodes, Egypt, or the tribes of Anatolia. Mehmed had two sons, Bayezid and Djem. Each sought to succeed his father, but Bayezid, with the support of the janissaries, reached Istanbul first and claimed the throne on 21

---

[200]"Dok. 68, Nga Drsh. i St. Magnos, 25 shkurt 1481," in *Dokumenta të shekullit XV*, vol. IV, pt. 1, p. 64; and Magno, *Annali Veneti*, p. 224.

[201]Pashazade, *Burime osmane*, pp. 231-232.

May 1481.[202] A civil war between the two brothers ensued. When Ahmed Gedik Pasha heard about the Sultan's death he realized that this news would strengthen the rebellion in Albania, so he took immediate measures to secure the main passes out of the country[203] to maintain his communications with Istanbul. Rumors of the Sultan's death had already begun circulating, making this task more difficult. Meanwhile, Bayezid recalled Ahmed Gedik Pasha from Albania, with the main body of his troops, to join him in the war against Djem in Anatolia. [204]

The Ottoman commander was reluctant to depart from Albania and abandon his expedition against Italy.[205] When he did attempt to leave, he encountered fierce opposition from the Albanian rebels who, armed with lances, blocked the main passes out of the country. After bitter fighting, Ahmed Gedik Pasha escaped from Albania on 1 June 1481, but,

---

[202]Tursun-Beg, *History of Mehmed the Conqueror*, p. 64; Brockman, *Two Sieges of Rhodes*, p. 92; and Fisher, *The Foreign Relations of Turkey, 1481-1512*, p. 16.

[203]Pashazade, in *Burime osmane*, p. 232.

[204]Inalcik, "Ahmed Pasha Gedik," p. 293; Fisher, *Foreign Relations of Turkey*, pp. 22, 29; and Simonde de Sismondi, *Histoire des républiques italiennes*, t. VII, pp. 183-184.

[205]Giovanni Maria degli Angiolelli, *Historia Turchesca, 1300-1514*, ed. Ion Ursu who mistakenly attributed the manuscript to Donado de Lezze, p. 171.

according to Ashik Pashazade, the Ottomans were forced to leave behind their animals and supplies.[206]

This marked a major victory for the rebels who very much needed weapons, supplies, and equipment. Following Ahmed's departure, the Albanian rebellion intensified and further disrupted communications between Vlora and Istanbul.[207] Even before the news of Mehmed's death reached Naples, the Albanian rebellion had attracted Ferrante's attention, and, for the first time since Scanderbeg's death, serious diplomatic contacts between Naples and Albania resumed.[208]

Rumors of Mehmed's death spread throughout Italy in late May, but it was not until the 29th that Venice received official confirmation of the fact.[209] Typically, communications between Venice and Istanbul took an average of 34 to 37 days,[210] but such important information as that of the Sul-

---

[206]Pashazade, *Burime osmane*, p. 233; and "Dok. 75, Nga letra e Rektorit dhe këshillit të Raguzës drejtuar mbretit të Siqilisë, 15 qershor 1481," in *Dokumenta të shekullit XV*, vol. IV, pt. 1, p. 68, which confirms that Ahmed Gedik Pasha left Albania on 1 June 1481.

[207]Pashazade, *Burime osmane*, p. 233.

[208]Islami and Frashëri, *Historia e popullit shqiptar*, vol. I, p. 293.

[209]Setton, *Papacy and the Levant*, vol. II, p. 371; and Simonde de Sismondi, *Histoire des républiques italiennes*, t. VIII, p. 184.

[210]For a discussion of the communications issue, see Treptow, "Distance and Communications," pp. 75-83.

tan's death traveled quickly, despite efforts by Bayezid's allies to suppress the news to allow him time to secure the
throne. Venice passed along the news of the mighty conqueror's death to the rest of Italy. Venetian envoys in Rome
confirmed rumors of Mehmed's death on 2 June. The following day, Sixtus IV ordered processions in Rome to celebrate the death of the great enemy of Christendom and conqueror of Constantinople.[211]

While the Italians rejoiced over the death of Mehmed
the Conqueror, his sons, Bayezid and Djem, engaged in a
bitter civil war for the right to succeed him. Their armies
met in battle on the plain of Yenishehir in Anatolia on 20
June 1481. Bayezid's forces, led by Ahmed Gedik Pasha, defeated Djem and forced him to flee to Mamluk territory.[212]
Although Djem made another futile attempt to gain the
throne in 1482,[213] this battle had, for all intents and purposes, decided the succession dispute in favor of Bayezid.

---

[211]Pastor, *History of the Popes*, vol. IV, p. 342; Setton, *Papacy and the Levant*,
vol. II, p. 371; and Simonde de Sismondi, *Histoire des républiques
italiennes*, t. VIII, p. 184.

[212]Halil Inalcik, "Djem," pp. 529-531 in *The Encyclopedia of Islam*, vol. II,
p. 529; and Fisher, *The Foreign Relations of Turkey*, p. 23.

[213]Fisher, *The Foreign Relations of Turkey*, pp. 26-27, 29.

For failing to capture Djem, Bayezid briefly imprisoned Ahmed Gedik Pasha, but popular pressure forced his release.[214]

Even before Djem's defeat and Ahmed Gedik Pasha's fall from favor at the Porte, Bayezid had appointed Suleiman Pasha Eunuch, the beylerbey of Rumelia, to take charge of the Italian expedition.[215] The death of Mehmed and the civil war between Bayezid and Djem had dealt serious blows to Ottoman efforts in Italy, but the damage was not irreparable. The Albanian rebellion, which had grown steadily since the departure of Ahmed Gedik Pasha and his troops, posed a serious threat to Suleiman's efforts to assist the Ottoman garrison at Otranto.

When Suleiman Pasha Eunuch reached Vlora in early June he faced a critical situation. The city was garrisoned by no more than 500 troops; an insufficient force to protect the unmanned Turkish fleet from a determined attack. The Ottoman predicament in Albania was well known. The Rector

---

[214]Inalcik, "Ahmed Gedik Pasha," p, 293; and Fisher, *The Foreign Relations of Turkey*, p. 27. Ahmed Gedik Pasha soon fell out of favor again with Bayezid and was executed in November, 1482.

[215]"Dok. 75, Nga letra e Rektorit dhe e këshillit të Raguzës drejtuar mbretit të Siqilisë, 15 qershor 1482," in *Dokumenta të shekullit XV*, vol. IV, pt. 1, p. 68.

of Ragusa wrote to Ferrante that the Turkish fleet at Vlora, "could easily be burned."[216]

The Albanian uprising threatened Ottoman positions throughout the country and interfered with Suleiman's efforts to relieve the garrison at Otranto, then under siege by Neapolitan and Papal forces. Instead of sending his troops to Italy, he had to keep them in Albania to reinforce the garrisons in the cities and fortresses under attack by the Albanian insurgents.

Suleiman understood that he could not cross the Adriatic before he secured his communication and supply lines through Albania. Several of the Albanian nobles who had fled to Italy following the Ottoman conquest of Albania saw the rebellion as an opportunity to return and to reclaim their former domains. This had an important impact on the Albanian revolt. Most of these men were experienced soldiers who could lend their leadership and military skills to the insurgents, while their ties to Italy could help bring much needed foreign financial and material assistance to the rebellion. On 2 June 1481, the Rector of Ragusa informed Fer-

---

[216]"Dok. 75, Nga letra e Rektorit dhe e këshillit të Raguzës drejtuar mbretit të Siqilisë, 15 qershor 1482," in *Dokumenta të shekullit XV*, vol. IV, pt. 1, p. 68.

rante that Prince Vlatku had returned to Bosnia and Nicholas Dukagjin to Albania to join in the armed movements in their former lands.[217]

The spread of the rebellion to neighboring lands further complicated matters for the Ottomans, as both Bosnia and Zeta rose in rebellion against Turkish domination. P. Gondolas wrote to Ferrante from Ragusa on 15 June that Lek Dukagjin had returned to Albania, while at the same time Ivan Crnojevic arrived in Zeta.[218] Ivan Crnojevic, a nephew of Scanderbeg, launched an attack on Zabliak, which had fallen to the Ottomans in 1477, regaining possession of this important fortress.[219]

The rebellions in Bosnia and Zeta further drained Ottoman manpower, but Albania remained the principal threat to the success of Turkish operations in Italy because the uprising there had disrupted the communication and supply lines upon which the invasion force was dependent. Long term success by the Albanian rebels, however, depended upon foreign assistance because the land lacked the man-

---

[217]"Dok. 74, Nga letra e Rektorit dhe këshillit të Raguzës drejtuar mbretit të Siqilisë, 2 qershor 1481, in *Dokumenta të shekullit XV*, vol. IV, pt. 1, p. 67.

[218]"Dok. 76, Nga letra e P. Gondolas drejtuar mbretit të Siqilisë, 15 qershor 1481," and confirmed in "Dok. 75, Nga letra e Rktorit dhe e këshillit të Raguzës drejtuar mbretit të Siqilisë, 15 qershor 1481," in *Dokumenta të shekullit XV*, vol. IV, pt. 1, p. 68.

[219]Stevenson, *A History of Montenegro*, p. 91.

power and resources to sustain an effective resistance movement. The Rector of Ragusa recognized this when he wrote
to Ferrante on 2 June 1481: "If there would be a little support, Bosnia and Albania could be able to exterminate the
Turks, since those people desire rebellion from their own
nature and from the fact that for a long time they suffered
from the heavy tyranny of the late Sultan. If there will be
delay, the attempts of Vlatku and Nicholas Dukagjin will be
in vain according to our judgement."[220]

This observation was not lost on the Neapolitans. Giovanni Albino, an aid to Duke Alfonso, wrote on 19 June that
it would be better to send additional naval reinforcements
to attack the Albanian coast instead of adding them to the
force blockading Otranto.[221]

Despite the arrival of Suleiman and his troops in Albania, the rebellion continued to intensify. In addition to
threatening Ottoman positions at Shkodra and Croya, the
insurgents also attacked Venetian possessions in Albania.[222]
Past experience had proven to the Albanian leaders that
long-term success in the anti-Ottoman struggle necessitated

---

[220]"Dok. 74, Nga letra e Rektorit dhe këshillit të Raguzës drejtuar mbretit
të Siqilisë, 2 qershor 1481, in *Dokumenta të shekullit XV*, vol. IV, pt. 1,
p. 67.

[221]"Dok. 37, Pjesë nga një letër drejtuar nga Pandolfo Albinos në lidhje
me rendisine qe ka bregdeti shqiptar për fatin e Otranto, 19 qershor
1481," in *Dokumente për Historine e Shqipërise, 1479-1506*, pt. II, pp. 68-69

[222]"Dok. 38, Pjesë nga një letër e Tomacelit drejtuar Albinos, 25 qershor
1481," in *Dokumente për Historine e Shqipërise, 1479-1506*, pt. II, p. 69.

having a unified command; thus, a delegation from the region of Himara, where the rebellion had originated, made its way to the Kingdom of Naples to ask Ferrante to grant permission for John Castriota, Scanderbeg's only son and lawful heir, to return to Albania and lead the insurgency.[223]

The choice of John Castriota to lead the revolt can be seen as a sign of cooperation amongst all elements of Albanian society. Only 27 years old at the time, he was not particularly experienced as a military leader. He had spent almost all of his adult life outside of Albania and thus could not even have had a good understanding of the geography of the country and the strategical and tactical possibilities which it offered and which his father had exploited with such great success over the years. The reason for his selection, however, lay in the fact that he was the legitimate heir of the great Scanderbeg. This made him a popular choice with the peasants who regarded Scanderbeg as their protector, while the fact that he was an aristocrat and vassal of the Neapolitan king also made him acceptable to the nobility.

When Scanderbeg died in January, 1468, John Castriota left Albania with his mother Donika. They settled in the Kingdom of Naples on the fiefs that Scanderbeg had received from King Ferrante for his assistance in helping him secure the Neapolitan throne against his Angevin rivals. At

---

[223]"Dok. 79, Nga Drsh. i St. Magno," in *Dokumenta të shekullit XV*, vol. IV, pt. 1, p. 70; Magno, *Annali Veneti*, p. 229; Rapo, "La lutte des Himariotes," p. 277; and *George Kastriot-Scanderbeg and the Albanian-Turkish War*, p. 129.

the time of the Albanian rebellion in 1481, John Castriota was serving in the army of the Duke of Calabria, which was then besieging Otranto.[224]

With the support of King Ferrante and Duke Alfonso, John Castriota returned to Albania in the summer of 1481 and assumed leadership of the rebellion. Once again, a member of the Castriota family would lead the Albanian people in their struggle to expel the Ottoman invaders. By supporting John Castriota's return to Albania, the Neapolitans hoped to further damage the Ottoman position in Italy.[225] As the Albanian historian Aleko Rapo has argued, "an Albanian insurrection not only would have impeded the subsequent advance of the Turks in Italy, but would also have facilitated their expulsion from the occupied citadel."[226]

The strong fortifications that Ahmed Gedik Pasha had installed at Otranto made the Neapolitan siege ineffective. In addition, because of the nature of galley warfare, the Christian fleet could not maintain absolute control of the sea. This made Ferrante's support of the Albanian uprising a strategic necessity, because, as John Guilmartin has

---

[224]Islami and Frashëri, *Historia e popullit shqiptar*, vol. I, p. 294; and Zamputi, "Gjon Kastrioti II (1454-pas 1502)," in *Fjalor Enciklopedik Shqiptar*, p. 461.

[225]Pontieri, *Ferrante d'Aragona re di Napoli*, p. 350.

[226]Rapo, "La lutte des Himariotes," p. 277.

pointed out, "In order to obtain decisive results the galley fleet had to capture the enemy fleet's bases."[227]

If the Albanian insurrection could render the Turkish base at Vlora useless by cutting off its communication and supply lines, the Ottoman garrison at Otranto would eventually be forced to capitulate. Thus, John Castriota's return to Albania received the full support of Ferrante who put four fully-manned and equipped galleys, commanded by Korkodeilos Kladas, an Albanian refugee from the Morea then in the service of the Neapolitan king, at his disposal.[228] With these galleys and a small force of Albanians, John Castriota embarked for his homeland to reclaim his inheritance.

Early in August, 1481, John Castriota and his men landed on the coast of northern Albania, south of Durrazo [Durres in Albanian]. He began to organize his campaign in the traditional lands of the Castriota family; meanwhile, Klada proceeded with the galleys, manned mostly by Albanians from the Morea, south along the coast, raiding Turkish positions along the way, until he reached Himara, south of Vlora, where he joined the Albanian rebels in their siege

---

[227]Guilmartin, *Gunpowder and Galleys*, p. 57.

[228]"Dok. 79, Nga Drsh. i St. Magno," in *Dokumenta të shekullit XV*, vol. IV, pt. 1, p. 70; Magno, *Annali Veneti*, p. 229; and Rapo, "La lutte des Himariotes," p. 277. Kladas had led a rebellion in Maina in the Morea which had been put down by the Turks in 1479. He then enetered into the service of Ferrante, see Setton, *Papacy and the Levant*, vol. II, pp. 328-329.

of that coastal fortress and base for the Ottoman invasion of Italy.[229]

When Suleiman received news that Castriota had landed, "[since he] was in Vlora to aid the city of Otranto," Venetian chronicler Stefano Magno relates, "[Suleiman] sent a sandjakbey of his, with 2,000 men, to the said land to expel him [John]."[230] John Castriota sent an advance force out to meet the Ottomans, but suffered a great defeat that resulted in the loss of many of his men. After this disaster, he considered returning to Puglia, but the Albanian insurgents rallied to his aid.

The rebel's prospects began to improve as a force of 6,000 infantrymen and 400 cavalrymen gathered around John Castriota, and he defeated a second Turkish force sent against him.

The Albanian rebellion in Himara posed the most serious threat to the Ottoman position in Vlora. Under the leadership of Konstantin Muzaka, the Himariotes, with the aid of Klada's galleys, besieged the coastal cities of Himara and

---

[229]"Dok. 79, Nga Drsh. i St. Magno," in *Dokumenta të shekullit XV*, vol. IV, pt. 1, p. 71; Magno, *Annali Veneti*, p. 229; and Rapo, "La lutte des Himariotes," p. 277.

[230]"Dok. 79, Nga Drsh. i St. Magno," in *Dokumenta të shekullit XV*, vol. IV, pt. 1, p. 71; and Magno, *Annali Veneti*, p. 229.

Sopot, surrounding them by land and sea.[231] Suleiman real-ized that so long as the Albanians threatened these strategi-cally important coastal positions south of Vlora, he could not send his troops to Italy. If these fortresses fell into rebel hands they could be used to launch attacks on Vlora by land and sea; they could also be used as bases from which to dis-rupt Ottoman shipping, which had to proceed north along the coast from Greece, and thereby threaten the provision-ing of the city by sea. Realizing the magnitude of the situa-tion, the Venetian chronicler Magno tells us that the Otto-man commander: "immediately set out with 3,000 Turks to go to assist [the Ottoman garrison at Himara], but against him, the people of the said mountain [the Himariotes], to-gether with many rowers of the said galleys, went to a mountain pass and defeated him and captured him [Sulei-man], together with many Turks, while they killed many others; the captured and the dead numbering around 1,000."[232]

The Ottomans had not only lost a significant number of men, but also the commander of the forces destined to relive the garrison at Otranto. This was a decisive victory because it eliminated any possibility that Suleiman would be able to

---

[231]"Dok. 79, Nga Drsh. i St. Magno," in *Dokumenta të shekullit XV*, vol. IV, pt. 1, p. 71; Magno, *Annali Veneti*, p. 229; and *George Kastriot-Scanderbeg and the Albanian-Turkish War*, p. 130.

[232]"Dok. 79, Nga Drsh. i St. Magno," in *Dokumenta të shekullit XV*, vol. IV, pt. 1, p. 72; and Magno, *Annali Veneti*, p. 229.

assist Turkish forces in Italy, thereby foreshadowing the re-capture of the city by the Neapolitans. It also meant that the Ottoman garrisons at Himara and Sopot could not count on any further relief efforts.

When the commander of the Ottoman garrison at Himara received news of Suleiman's defeat, Magno informs us that: "[he] abandoned the said fortress of Himara, and took a barge to Corfu where he arrived on the day of 31 August. As he abandoned that place, the aforesaid Klada, who was with the said galleys. entered it, and then he also went on to take the fortress of Sopot which was also in the said mountains."[233]

The victories at Himara and Sopot, combined with John Castriota's defeat of the Turkish forces sent against him in central Albania, marked the pinnacle of the Albanian rebellion of 1481. John Castriota was recognized as Prince of Albania and the Himariotes presented the captured Ottoman commander, Suleiman Pasha Eunuch, to him. Castriota then turned over Suleiman to the Duke of Calabria in return for an additional 4,000 ducats to help finance the uprising in

---

[233]"Dok. 79, Nga Drsh. i St. Magno," in *Dokumenta të shekullit XV*, vol. IV, pt. 1, p. 72; and Magno, *Annali Veneti*, p. 229.

Albania,[234] while the Neapolitans also sent provisions to the newly won fortress of Himara.[235]

The Albanian victories over Suleiman and his troops, combined with the subsequent capture of Himara and Sopot came at a critical moment for Ferrante. Financial difficulties hampered the Neapolitan efforts to recover Otranto. After Mehmed's death, most Christians believed that the danger posed by the Ottomans had passed, and thus they were reluctant to assist the Neapolitan king. The inability to penetrate the Ottoman fortifications had nearly broken the morale of his troops, while the outbreak of the plague on four of the galleys and mutinies because the crews had not been paid, led the Neapolitan and Papal fleets to consider abandoning the blockade of Otranto at the beginning of September.[236]

Intending to use Otranto as a base for future expansion into Italy, Ahmed Gedik Pasha had significantly improved the city's fortifications immediately after its capture; he left

---

[234]"Dok. 79, Nga Drsh. i St. Magno," in *Dokumenta të shekullit XV*, vol. IV, pt. 1, p. 72; and Magno, *Annali Veneti*, p. 229.

[235]"Dok. 39, Alfonsi, duka I Kalabrise, I jep instruksione Albinos qe të nisët për Himarë e të marre në dore punët e kesaje krahine, 7 shtator 1481," in *Dokumente për Historine e Shqipërise, 1479-1506*, pt. II, pp. 70-74.

[236]Pastor, *History of the Popes*, vol. IV, p. 345. According to Setton it cost 4,000 ducats to man and equip a galley for six months, see *Papacy and the Levant*, vol. II, p. 368. This figure coincides with the documentary evidence which indicates that the Papal Consistory allocated 100,000 ducats to equip a fleet of 25 galleys.

a well-provisioned garrison that could hold out through the winter of 1481-1482, if necessary, so long as there remained a possibility of receiving assistance from Vlora. Thus, at the beginning of September, 1481, Neapolitan prospects at Otranto appeared tenuous at best.

Ferrante had hoped that the death of Mehmed the Conqueror would bring an end to the Ottoman occupation of Otranto. It was not to be. Despite Neapolitan efforts to bribe the Ottoman garrison shortly after Mehmed's death, the Turks held out. Alfonso hired additional mercenaries and brought in artillery when he began the siege of Otranto in June, and the papal fleet, commanded by Cardinal Paolo di Campofregoso, joined the Neapolitan fleet in an attempt to blockade the city.

Once he had surrounded Otranto by land and sea, Duke Alfonso ordered an assault on the city, but the fortifications proved too strong and the Neapolitans suffered heavy casualties.[237] Christian morale had reached its lowest point when news of the Albanian successes arrived in Italy. This breathed new life into the Christian efforts, and the situation soon reversed itself. The defeat of Suleiman Pasha Eunuch, and the capture of Himara and Sopot, ended any hopes that support would reach the Ottoman garrison at Otranto. Realizing the precarious nature of their position, on 10 September 1481, less than two weeks after the Albanians captured

---

[237]Cambini, *Two Commentaries*, p. 37; Gegaj, *L'Albanie et l'invasion turque*, p. 155; Pastor, *History of the Popes*, vol. IV, p. 343; and Setton, *Papacy and the Levant*, vol. II, p. 371.

Himara, the Ottoman forces in Italy surrendered to the Duke of Calabria.[238]

Several of the captured Turkish battalions entered into the service of Duke Alfonso and were later employed in the Italian Wars.[239] What had begun as a major expedition to extend Ottoman domination into Italy, ended in a whimper as a dramatic confrontation between the forces of Islam and Christendom never occurred on Italian soil. Events across the Adriatic had been decisive in determining the outcome of the Ottoman-Neapolitan conflict in Italy.

News of the recapture of Otranto reached Rome on 18 September 1481. Sixtus IV had intended for the papal fleet to carry the war across the Adriatic to join the Albanians in attacking Ottoman positions on the coast.[240] He hoped to use the opportunity presented by the defeat of the Ottomans at Otranto to organize a crusade against the Turkish Infidels and immediately issued appeals to the Christian leaders of Europe to undertake this holy cause.[241] The general Christian attitude about crusading in the late fifteenth century

---

[238]Islami and Frashëri, *Historia e popullit shqiptar*, vol. I, p. 294; Setton, *Papacy and the Levant*, vol. II, p. 371; and Pastor, *History of the Popes*, vol. IV, p. 343.

[239]Simonde de Sismondi, *Histoire des républiques italiennes*, t. VIII, p. 184.

[240]Pastor, *History of the Popes*, vol. IV, p. 344. Sixtus IV expressed his desire for a crusade in a letter to Genoa dated 30 August 1481.

[241]"Doc. 64, Pope Sixtus IV to Duke Philibert I of Savoy, 18 September 1481," in Pastor, *History of the Popes*, vol. IV, p. 518.

was embodied in the action of the Portuguese. When news of the recovery of Otranto reached Rome, there were 25 Portuguese ships preparing to leave for Otranto to join the Neapolitan and Papal fleets, but, upon hearing the news, they lost interest in the expedition and returned home.[242]

Although the Italian peninsula had narrowly escaped Islamic conquest, thanks in large measure to the Albanian across the narrow sea, the appeals of Pope Sixtus IV fell on deaf ears. The age of crusading had ended; Europe, having largely ceded the southeastern part of the continent to the forces of Islam, now concentrated on its own affairs.

Upon receiving the news about Otranto, Sixtus IV sent instructions to Cardinal Campofregoso, Legate of the Papal fleet, to proceed across the Adriatic and follow up the victory at Otranto.[243] Ferrante likewise agreed that the Christian forces should take advantage of Ottoman troubles and seize the offensive. He would have liked to free Albania from Ottoman control and make it a defensive barrier to protect southern Italy from future attacks;[244] this had been the policy followed by Ferrante's father, Alfonso V, when he aided Scanderbeg against the Ottomans in the 1450s. Support for these grandiose plans, however, could not be found. The surrender of the Ottoman garrison at Otranto

---

[242]Pastor, *History of the Popes*, vol. IV, p. 344.

[243]"Doc. 65, Pope Sixtus IV to Cardinal Fregoso, Legate of the Crusader Fleet, 18 September 1481," in Pastor, *History of the Popes*, vol. IV, p. 519.

[244]Pontieri, *Ferrante d'Aragona*, pp. 350-351.

had done little to improve Christian morale because the plague remained a persistent threat and the soldiers remained without pay. Also, winter was rapidly approaching, making the logistics of such a campaign extremely difficult. To add to the already serious financial difficulties of the Christian forces, the Ottoman artillery had inflicted heavy damage on the Neapolitan and Papal fleets at Otranto before surrendering; at least 40,000 ducats would be needed for repairs.[245]

Complicating matters further, Ferrante and the Pope remained at odds, despite their cooperation in the recovery of Otranto. While Sixtus IV appealed for united action against the Turks in September, 1481, he was already secretly preparing to go to war with Ferrante over Ferrara;[246] by the spring of the following year, the Pope had again become an ally of the Venetians, who themselves had refused to celebrate the Ottoman defeat at Otranto,[247] and was at war with Naples and Ferrara. Such was the nature of Italian politics in the fifteenth century. All this combined to prevent the Christian forces from taking the offensive and carrying the war against Islam across the straits of Otranto.

John Castriota continued his efforts to liberate Albania after the fall of Otranto. He captured the fortress of

---

[245]Pastor, *History of the Popes*, vol. IV, p. 347.

[246]Pastor, *History of the Popes*, vol. IV, p. 349; and Bentley, *Politics and Culture*, pp. 29-30

[247]Vespasiano da Bisticci, *Renaissance Princes, Popes, and Prelates*, p. 152.

Stelushit, but an attack on his father's old capital, Croya, failed.[248] While the restored Albanian principality included more lands than Scanderbeg had had under his control, its foundation was much weaker. The cities, with the exceptions already noted, remained in the hands of Ottoman and Venetian garrisons, and significant foreign assistance to the Albanians was not forthcoming. The harsh winter of the Albanian mountains protected the insurgents until the following spring when Ottoman forces returned, and, with help from renegade Albanian nobles, put down the rebellion, except in the Himara region.

With the collapse of the rebellion, John Castriota returned to Naples, never to see his homeland again.[249] The Himariotes continued to defy the Ottomans from their mountain stronghold, with the help of some material support from Naples,[250] but the peace treaty concluded in 1483

[248]"Dok. 79, Nga Drsh. i St. Magno," in *Dokumenta të shekullit XV*, vol. IV, pt. 1, pp. 71-73; Magno, *Annali Veneti*, p. 229; and Zamputi, "Gjon Kastrioti II (1454-pas 1502), p. 461.

[249]"Dok. 95, Letër e mbretit të Napolit drejtuar birit të Skenderbeut, Gjon Kastrioti, 17 shtator 1483," in in *Dokumenta të shekullit XV*, vol. IV, pt. 1, pp. 84-85, which confirms that John Castriota had returned to the Kingdom of Naples before that date.

[250]"Dok. 39, Alfonsi, duka i Kalabrise, I jep instruksione Albinos qe te niset për Himarë e te marre në dore punet e kesaj krahine, 7 shtator 1481," in *Dokumente për Historine e Shqipërise, 1479-1506*, pt. II, pp. 70-74.

between Ferrante and the Sultan isolated them. Their re-sistance continued until 1484 when Himara again fell under Ottoman control.[251]

Although the rebellion of 1481 failed to achieve its goal of liberating the land from the Ottoman yoke, it was a sig-nificant event in Albanian history. It formed part of a long series of struggles by the Albanian people against foreign oppression and shaped a spirit of independence that re-mained in the Albanian consciousness throughout nearly four hundred and fifty years of Ottoman rule. While travel-ing in Albania in 1879, the English barrister Edward Knight observed: "[The Turks] seem, even after so many centuries, to be merely temporarily encamped in Albania. They have pachas and garrisons in the towns, but the natives enjoy a surprising amount of independence, and are allowed to do pretty well as they like. Indeed, the government is very weak here, neither feared nor respected – merely toler-ated."[252]

The important contribution of Scanderbeg's rebellion and the subsequent Albanian resistance to the Turks should not be underestimated. It helped to preserve the Albanian ethnic identity throughout the centuries of Ottoman domi-nation. The Albanian rebellion of 1481 also marked an im-portant moment in European history. Mehmed II could only

---

[251]Islami and Frashëri, *Historia e popullit shqiptar*, p. 296; and *George Kastriot-Scanderbeg and the Albanian-Turkish War*, p. 131.

[252]Knight, *Albania*, p. 116.

launch his attack on Italy after the subjugation of Albania and the conclusion of the peace between Venice and the Porte in January, 1479; control of this area being a necessary prerequisite for the Ottoman expedition. Therefore, the success of Turkish efforts in Italy depended upon maintaining this control. In planning this expedition, however, the Ottomans did not adequately prepare for this contingency. Albanian historian Aleko Rapo has correctly argued that, "After having broken the first resistance of our people, the Turks prepared to extend their conquests in Europe, without evaluating the danger that the mountain zones of Albania still presented to their rear."[253]

Thus, when the Albanian rebellion broke out in 1481, it caught the Ottomans unprepared and forced them to keep troops and supplies in Albania that otherwise would have went to relieve Otranto. In this respect, the Albanian rebellion of 1481 can be seen as having helped define the limits of Ottoman expansion in this direction, as the Adriatic Sea came to delineate the boundary between Islam and Christianity in this region. It also marked the end of an effective, organized opposition to Ottoman domination in Albania. Nearly forty years after he had raised the red banner with the black double-headed eagle over Croya, the epoch of Scanderbeg had finally come to an end.

The resistance to Ottoman expansion in Albania, inspired and led by Scanderbeg, left a permanent mark upon

---

[253]Rapo, "La lutte des Himariotes," p. 277.

the people of this land. In essence, it was a conservative movement, aimed at preserving independence and a traditional way of life. It lacked a social or class basis. Nevertheless, the necessities of war transformed it into something revolutionary, for a sense of unity was forged amongst a people, up to now loosely bound by a common language and culture, but little else. By creating this unbreakable sense of solidarity, the anti-Ottoman struggle from 1443-1481 planted the seeds of a national consciousness that would be harvested centuries later by great Albanian national leaders such as Naum Veqilhardji, the Frashëri brothers, and others.

George Castriota Scanderbeg

Epilogue

*"Thou, O Padishah, knowest well the great dis-
sensions that are raging in Italy especially, and in
all Frankistan [Christian Europe] generally. In
consequence of these dissensions the Gaiours [In-
fidels] are incapable of united action against us.
The Christian potentates will never unite together. When, after protracted efforts, they conclude something like a peace among themselves, it
never lasts long. Even when they are bound by
treaties of alliance, they are not prevented from
seizing territories from each other. They always
stand in fear of each other, and are busily occupied
in intriguing against each other. No doubt they
think much, speak much, and explain much, but
after all they do very little. When they decide to do
anything, they waste much time before they begin
to act. Suppose they have even commenced something. They cannot progress very far with it because they are sure to disagree amongst themselves how to proceed..."*

— Zagan Pasha to Mehmed the Conqueror,
27 May 1453[254]

Zagan Pasha's speech before the walls of Constantinople, encouraging the Sultan to order an all-out assault on the

---

[254]quoted in L.S. Stavrianos, *The Balkans since 1453*, p. 58.

city, provides an apt description of the situation confronting George Castriota Scanderbeg and the Albanian people as they sought help from the states of Christian Europe in their struggle to defend themselves from the Islamic invasion. This struggle would define the Albanians as a people. Likewise, the ultimate failure of their efforts would symbolize the fate of this region of Europe. Nearly half a millennium of Ottoman domination would leave its mark on Albanian society – the results of which can still be seen today.

Although Albania fell to the Turks, the struggle led by Scanderbeg helped to save Europe from a similar fate. One of the reasons for his success was the fact that young George had been educated at the Sultan's court. This fact would be of vital importance, as the Serbian Janissary, Konstantin Mihailović, observed: "it is far easier for one to defend himself against the Turks who is familiar with them than for one who does not know their customs."[255]

Although Scanderbeg was not a social revolutionary, his actions, dictated purely by military necessity, had a radical impact on the socio-economic structure of Albania. Scanderbeg had to attempt to create the state institutions necessary to ensure the independence of his country, which had not yet come into existence prior to the period of Ottoman expansion in Europe.

This goal of affirming the independence of his country also dictated the Albanian leader's foreign policy. Although

---

[255]Mihailović, *Memoirs of a Janissary*, p. 135.

he would both become renowned for his fierce resistance to Ottoman expansion, his foreign policy, aimed at protecting his independence, led him into conflicts with Christian powers as well, namely Venice.

Religion was not the primary motivation in pursuing the struggle against Ottoman expansion. Albania was on the borders of the Catholic and Orthodox worlds, yet organized religion played a limited role in Albanian society. When considering the question of the struggle of Christianity against Islam in fifteenth century Europe, it is essential to recall the failure of the Union proclaimed by the Council of Florence in 1439, like similar attempts before it, to resolve the deep rupture between the Catholic and Orthodox worlds. As L.S. Stavrianos pointed out, "each agreement for union proved meaningless in the face of the undying hatred of the Orthodox Greeks for the Catholic Latins – a hatred intensified by the barbarities of the Fourth Crusade and the merciless stranglehold of the Italian merchants."[256] For peoples throughout the Orthodox world, the cry "Better Islam than the Pope!" was more than just a slogan.

This is not to underestimate the importance of religion in the system of international relations of the time. Religion served as a weapon of diplomacy. Pope Calixtus III replied to Scanderbeg, when he appealed to the Holy See for support in his struggle against the Ottomans, exhorting the Albanian leader to: "Continue to defend the Catholic faith;

---

[256]Stavrianos, *The Balkans since 1453*, p. 56.

God, for whom you fight, will not abandon his cause."[257] Religion affected every aspect of life in medieval times and this is no less true of diplomacy.

Ultimately the anti-Ottoman resistance led by Scanderbeg failed. The reasons for his failure are complex. One was the failure of strong state institutions to develop in this part of Europe. Albania was unprepared to face the threat posed by Islamic expansion. Interference from neighboring powers, who sought to preserve these weak institutions, both to protect their own interests in these regions, as well as to use these lands as buffer states to stave off the threat posed by the extension of Islam into Southeastern Europe, further inhibited the creation of a strong state formation. The problem of foreign interference, however, is a double-edged sword. On the one hand, outside threats helped to promote the consolidation of state formations, on the other hand, if the threat was too great it could stifle the development of native institutions. The important elements in this calculation are the degree of the threat and at what point in the development of the state it appeared.

An additional reason for the failure of strong state institutions to develop in Albania was the strength of peasant organization in the Balkans. The basically agricultural societies of Southeastern Europe had a long tradition of communal organization, as we saw in the example of the Slavic

---

[257]quoted in Pastor, *History of the Popes*, vol. II, p. 434.

zadruga. These were, in essence, extended family organizations whose way of life was based on custom and tradition. While it would be a strong, effective form of social organization for Balkan society during the early Middle Ages, it would also inhibit the development of the strong state institutions necessary to confront the Ottoman threat and have serious consequences for the future social and economic development of the region.

Although the Albanians are not a Slavic people, the impact of Slavic culture on all aspects of life cannot be denied. In this respect, one of the most important aspects was the Slavic customary law of equal division of inheritances among male offspring and the lack of primogeniture. As Philip Longworth pointed out, when analyzing the causes for the underdevelopment of Eastern Europe, "These arrangements were conducive to the maintenance of peace within the family, the village and the clan, but their effectiveness was predicated on a low population and relatively plentiful resources, conditions that were not to last. In the long term the consequences of these customary understandings were profound and largely adverse; and they took political and cultural, as well as economic forms."[258]

The lack of primogeniture would have a serious impact upon the development of state institutions and, in later cen-

---

[258]Longworth, *The Making of Eastern Europe*, p. 300.

turies, for village life as well. In Albania, it helped to continue the divisive nature of society by inhibiting the consolidation of powers and territories.

Another aspect of Slavic customary law that had a neg-
ative impact on state development was the principle that a
ruler was not bound by the acts of his predecessors. It prevented the development of a civic society, based on law, and
created anxiety and instability in political and social life. In
addition, it would have serious economic consequences as
property rights failed to be established on any sort of legal,
contractual basis; an essential element for the evolution of a
mercantile or capitalist system of economic relations.

Thus, we can conclude that the weakness of institu-
tional development is directly responsible for the failure to
organize a strong defense against the Ottoman threat, making it a principal cause for the failure of the resistance led by
George Castriota Scanderbeg in Albania.

Another cause would be the failure of the Christian
states of Europe to organize against the Ottoman threat. The
analysis of Sultan's General, Zagan Pasha, is valid for the
situation all throughout this period. Every effort at organizing a Christian offensive to halt the expansion of Ottoman
power would be doomed to failure for the reasons cited by
Zagan Pasha as he urged Mehmed to order the final, decisive assault on the walls of the Byzantine capital in May,
1453. Meanwhile, the centralized political and military or-

ganization of the Ottomans, based on a militant Islamic religious ideology, would propel the expansion of the Empire as they continued their advance into Europe.

In Albania, Venetian economic exploitation created a socio-economic basis for resistance to foreign interference. While Scanderbeg gave leadership and guidance to this movement, he did not create it. Scanderbeg led a popular resistance to Ottoman expansion in Albania, no state structure had come into existence in that land; there was no administrative apparatus. This is something that, as we have seen, the Albanian leader would have to overcome in trying to organize an effective opposition to Ottoman expansion. This was first attempted through the organization of the League of Alessio, but later Castriota came to realize that only through strong personal control could maintain an effective military force. As a consequence of the lack of any form of centralized government, we have no internal documents from fifteenth century Albania. Our analysis of the Albanian struggle against Islamic expansion is, out of necessity, based on memoirs, chronicles, and diplomatic correspondence from the time.

Albania was important politically because it was located on the border between East and West. Control of Albania was critical for an eventual Islamic attack on Italy. As a result, after the Ottoman conquest, the Porte established direct rule in the Balkans. The establishment of direct Ottoman rule in southeastern Europe would have a decisive impact on the future social and economic development of Albania. The Ottoman system of economic exploitation would establish a feudal-military economic system in this region. Thus, while feudalism was breaking down in Western Europe, it emerged from the turmoil of the fifteenth century, aided by the installation of Ottoman rule in the region, and persisted throughout the following centuries.

The installation of Ottoman rule in southeastern Europe also had another devastating consequence; it closed off prosperous trading routes between East and West. Instead of being located along important commercial routes that brought with them a certain degree of prosperity, the lands of southeastern Europe, including Albania, became marginalized in the European economy. As an "Iron Curtain" between the Christian and Islamic worlds was erected, commerce came to a halt. Trade with the Orient would henceforth be conducted over sea routes; a change symbolized by the discovery of America at the end of the fifteenth century. Thus, the installation of the Ottoman regime would be decisive for the future social and economic development of the region.

We cannot, however, accept any deterministic view of these events. Despite conditions that facilitated the Islamic advance into the region, including the existence of various factors that created a political vacuum in southeastern Europe prior to their arrival, the Ottoman conquest was not inevitable. Had the Christian states of Europe made a concerted, well-coordinated effort, they could have halted the

Ottoman advance. Had the unification of the Polish and Hungarian crowns, realized for a brief time (1440-1444) under King Ladislas, continued, it could have led to other results. Had the Ottomans not succeeded in overcoming their own internal conflicts at the beginning of the century, the Empire could very well have faded away like the Mongol Empire before it. Had the Ottoman royal family not produced several capable and determined leaders it would have failed to assert its dominance in this region. These speculations all pose questions outside of the scope of historical study where we are obliged to concentrate on what happened and why. We only mention them here to remind ourselves, as we analyze why things happened the way they did, and the impact they had on the future, that resistance to Islamic expansion in southeastern Europe was by no means futile and that things could have had another outcome.

Although the resistance to Ottoman expansion led by Scanderbeg ultimately failed, he was also victorious and his actions had important repercussions for the history of his people. The events that we have described are largely the results of actions by individuals who consciously chose to follow a particular course of action. While confronted with a certain set of conditions, these realities did not, and never do, impose a single course of action. Thus, the actions of leaders such as Scanderbeg have consequences.

Without a leader of George Castriota's caliber, the Albanian resistance to Islamic expansion into southeastern Europe would have ended by the mid-fifteenth century. He breathed new life into a movement that was rapidly dissipating. His resistance ultimately protected Italy from an invasion by Mehmed the Conqueror who only managed to make such an attempt during the last year of his life. Had Mehmed been able to launch this invasion earlier, he may have succeeded in subduing Rome in the same way that he had earlier conquered Constantinople.

Scanderbeg's resistance also forged a sense of unity and created a legend that would remain alive in the memory of his people for centuries to come. During the years of Ottoman domination, Albanian folk songs and oral traditions kept alive the memory of his resistance to the Turks. He became the focus of an ethnic identity, reinforcing the Albanian realization that they were a distinct group of people with a unique heritage. For example, in 1636, Frang Bardhi, an Albanian bishop, published *George Castriota of Epirus, generally named Scanderbeg, very brave and invincible Prince of the Albanians* to refute the claim of a Bosnian bishop that Scanderbeg was of Slavic and not Albanian origin.[259]

The resistance to the Ottomans, led by Scanderbeg, forged a sense of unity among his people. Unlike other Balkan peoples, such as the Bulgarians or Serbs, Albanians did

---

[259]Koli Xoxe, "Frang Bardhi (1606-1643)," in *Fjalor Enciklopedik Shqiptar*, p. 68.

Frontispiece

Scanderbeg

not have a medieval state formation to look back upon and long for its revival. The struggle against Islamic expansion led by Scanderbeg would be the defining moment in the medieval history of the Albanian people. Even for peasants in those areas of the country that did not participate in his revolt, as we have seen in the case of Himara in 1481, Scanderbeg symbolized their fight against foreign oppression and they kept his memory alive. Four and a half centuries of Ottoman rule could not destroy the sense of ethnic unity that his resistance helped to forge during the fifteenth century. This strong sense of ethnic awareness, of which the memory of Scanderbeg's resistance formed an important part, created the basis for the development of an Albanian national consciousness during the nineteenth century.[260]

History was one of the prominent concerns of the Albanian intellectuals who fostered the awakening of national consciousness among their people. There were two prominent issues in nineteenth century Albanian historiography. One was the question of the origins of the Albanian people, aimed at demonstrating their Illyrian origin and proving that they were among the oldest inhabitants of the Balkan peninsula. The other was George Castriota Scanderbeg and his famous resistance to Ottoman domination. Nineteenth century intellectuals saw in Scanderbeg an example for their own century, for uniting their people together in a common

---

[260]Treptow, "The Formation of the Albanian National Consciousness," in *From Zalmoxis to Jan Palach*, pp. 91-93.

struggle against foreign domination. Scanderbeg's struggle came to symbolize the ethnic unity of the people that these intellectuals wished to propagate. It also served their political goals; by emphasizing the Albanian resistance to the Ottomans they found a means of refuting the view prevalent in Europe at that time that they were Turks. Many of the patriotic leaders of the nineteenth century wrote works about Scanderbeg. The most important of these include Zef Jubani's *History of the Life and Deeds of George Castriota Scanderbeg,*[261] published in 1878, Jeronim De Rada's *The Unlucky Scanderbeg,* published in 1884,[262] and Naim Frasheri's epic poem, *The History of Scanderbeg,* published in 1898.[263]

Pashko Vasa used the example of Scanderbeg to emphasize the distinction between Albanians and Greeks. The fact that the Greeks did not assist Scanderbeg in his struggle against the Ottoman invaders, he argued, proved that the Albanians formed a distinct ethnic group.[264]

The efforts of these men to make Scanderbeg a focal point for the developing Albanian national consciousness

[261]Jup Kastrati, "Zef Jubani (1818-1880)," in *Fjalor Enciklopedik Shqiptar,* p. 436; and Pollo, ed., *Historisë e Shqipërisë,* vol. II, p. 165.

[262]Jeronim De Rada, "Skanderbeku I pafan," in *Jeronim De Rada, Vepra Letrare,* vol. II; and Koço Bihiku, *A History of Albanian Literature,* pp. 80-81.

[263]Dhimitër Shuteriqi, "Naim Frashëri (1846-1900)," in *Fjalor Enciklopedik Shqiptar,* p. 289.

[264]Wassa Effendi (Pashko Vasa), *Études sur l'Albanie et les Albanais,* p. 45.

were successful. Edith Durham, a British anthropologist who traveled in Albania at the beginning of the twentieth century, confirmed this, remarking that "Scanderbeg is a great hero in his own land."[265]

When the independent Albanian nation-state was created in 1912, the flag of Scanderbeg, a black double-headed eagle on a red background, was adopted as the national flag of the newly born country. It has remained so ever since. Thus, the resistance led by Scanderbeg would be a defining moment in the history of the Albanian people that would plant a seed to be reaped by later generations.

---

[265]Mary Edith Durham, *The Burden of the Balkans*, p. 309.

Bibliography

Ady, Cecilia. "The Invasions of Italy," pp. 343-367 in *The New Cambridge Modern History, Volume 1: The Renaissance, 1493-1520*. Ed. G.R. Potter. Cambridge: Cambridge University Press, 1967

Anderson, Perry. *Passages from Antiquity to Feudalism*. London: Verso Editions, 1978.

Armstrong, Edward. "The Papacy and Naples in the Fifteenth Century," pp. 158-201 in *The Cambridge Medieval History, Volume 8: The Close of the Middle Ages*. Eds. C.W. Previté-Orton and Z.N. Brooke. Cambridge: Cambridge University Press, 1936.

Armstrong, William J. *The Heroes of Defeat*. Cincinnati: The Robert Clarke Company, 1905.

Arnold, T.W. *The Preaching of Islam: A History of the propagation of the Muslim Faith*. New York: Charles Scribner's Sons, 1913.

Aston, T.H. and C.H.E. Philpin. *The Brenner Debate: Agrarian Class Structure and Economic Development in Pre-Industrial Europe*. Cambridge: Cambridge University Press, 1985.

Babinger, Franz. *Mehmed the Conqueror and His Time*. Trans. Ralph Manheim. Ed. William C. Hickman. Princeton: Princeton University Press, 1978.

Barleci, Marin. *Rrethimi i Shkodrës*. Tiranë, 1961.

Barleti, Marin. *Historia e jetës dhe e vepravet të Skënderbeut*. Ed. Stefan I. Prifti. Tiranë, 1967.

Bentley, Jerry H. *Politics and Culture in Renaissance Naples*. Princeton: Princeton University Press, 1987.

Biçoku, Kasem. "Quelques aspects des rapports entre Skanderbeg et Venise," in *Studia Albanica*, 5:1 (1968), pp. 95-102.

Bihiku, Koço. *History of Albanian Literature*. Tirana, 1980.

Bihiku, Koço. *An Outline of Albanian Literature*. Trans. Ali Cungu. Tirana: The «Naim Frashëri» State Publishing House, 1964.

Birge, John Kingsley. *The Bektashi Order of Dervishes*. London: Luzac & Co. Ltd., 1965.

Bisticci, Vespasiano da. *Renaissance Princes, Popes, and Prelates: The Vespasiano Memoirs, Lives of the Illustious Men of the XVth Century*. Trans. William George and Emily Waters. New York, 1963.

Bois, Guy. *The Crisis of Feudalism: Economy and Society in Eastern Normandy c. 1300-1550*. Cambridge: Cambridge University Press, 1984.

Bozhari, Koço and Filip Liço. *Burime tregimtare Bizantine për historinë e Shqipërisë, shek. X-XV*. Tiranë: Akademia e Shkencave e RPSh, Instituti i Historisë, 1975.

Braudel, Fernand. *The Mediterranean and the Mediterranean World in the Age of Philip II*. 2 volumes. Trans. Siân Reynolds. New York: Harper and Row Publishers, 1973.

Brockman, Eric. *The Two Sieges of Rhodes, 1480-1522*. London, 1969.

A Brief Account of the Life and Charavcter of George Castriot, King of Epirus and Albania, Commonly called Scanderbeg. London: J. Roberts, 1735.

Buda, Aleks. *Fjalor Enciklopedik Shqiptar*. Tiranë, 1985.

Buda, Aleks. "Georges Kastriote-Skanderbeg et son epoque," in *Studia Albanica*, 4:2 (1967), pp. 3-29.

Buda, Aleks. "La place des Albanais dans l'histoire européene des VIIIe-XVIIIe siècles," in *Studia Albanica*, 4:1 (1967), pp. 21-38.

Burime të zgjedhura për Historinë e Shqipërisë, vëll. II, shek. VIII-XV. Ed. Kristo Frashëri. Tiranë: Universiteti shtetëror i Tiranës, 1962.

Cambini, Andrea. *Two Commentaries the One of the Originall of the Turcks thother of the Warre of the Turcke against George Scanderbeg*. London, 1562. Reprint: Amstersdam, 1970.

Byron, Lord. *Childe Harold's Pilgrimage*. Ed. William J. Rolfe. Boston and New York: Houghton, Mifflin & Company, 1899.

Cambridge Medieval History, Volume IV: The Byzantine Empire, Part 1 — Byzantium and its Neighbors. Ed. J.M. Hussey. Cambridge: At the University Press, 1966.

Cambridge Medieval History, Volume IV: The Eastern Roman Empire (717-1453). Ed. J.R. Tanner. Cambridge: At the University Press, 1936.

Cambridge Medieval History, Volume VIII: The Close of the Middle Ages. Eds. C.W. Previté-Orton and Z.N. Brooke. Cambridge: At the University Press, 1936.

Castellan, Georges. *L'Albanie*. Paris: Presses Universitaires de France, 1980.

Chalcocondil, Laonic. *Expuneri istorice*. Trans. Vasile Grecu. Bucureşti: Editura Academiei, 1958.

Chatzidakis, Manolis and André Grabar. *Byzantine and Early Medieval Painting*. New York: Viking Press, 1965.

Chekrezi, Constantine A. *Albania: Past and Present*. New York: The MacMillan Company, 1919.

Chirot, Daniel. *Social Change in a Peripheral Society: The Creation of a Balkan Colony*. New York: Academic Press, 1976.

"The Code of Stephan Dušan." Trans. Malcom Burr. Part I in *The Slavonic and East European Review*, 28:70 (November, 1949), pp. 198-217; Part II in *The Slavonic and East European Review*, 29:71 (April, 1950), pp. 516-539.

Da Lezze, Donado [Giovanni Maria degli Angiolelli]. *Historia Turchesca (1300-1514)*. Ed. Ion Ursu. Bucureşti: Ediţiunea Academiei Române, 1909.

Church, Richard William. *Miscellaneous Essays*. London and New York: MacMillan & Co., 1888.

Cleray, Edouard. "Le voyage de Pierre Lescalopier Parisien de Venise à Constantinople, l'an 1574," in *Revue d'histoire diplomatique*, 35 (1921), pp. 21-55.

Cross, Geoffrey Neale. *Epirus: A Study in Greek Constitutional Development*. Cambridge: Cambridge University Press, 1932.

Daru, Le Comte. *Histoire de Venise*. Volume I. Bruxelles, 1838.

Davenport, R.A. *The Life of Ali Pasha, of Tepeleni, Vizier of Epirus: Surnamed Aslan or the Lion*. London: Thomas Tegg and Son, 1837.

Decei, Aurel. *Istoria Imperiului Otoman pînă la 1656.* București: Editura Științifică și Enciclopedică, 1978.

De Rada, Jeronim. *Vepra Letrare.* 3 volumes. Ed. Jup Kastrati. Tiranë, 1987.

D'Istria, Dora. "La nationalité Albanaise selon les chants populaires," in *Revue des deux mondes,* 68 (May-June, 1866), pp. 382-418.

Dobb, Maurice. *Studies in the Development of Capitalism.* New York: International Publishers, 1984.

Drishti, Riza. "L'utilisation des armes à feu par les troupes de Skanderbeg," in *Studia Albanica,* 5:1 (1968), pp. 177-180.

Dokumenta të shekullit XV për historinë e Shqipërisë, vëll. 4 (1479-1506), pjesa 1 (1479- 1499). Ed. Injac Zamputi. Tirana, 1967.

Dokumente për historinë e Shqipërisë të shek. XV, vëll. I (1400-1405). Ed. Aleks Buda. Tiranë, 1987.

Dokumente për historinë e Shqipërisë, 1479-1506, pjesa e dyte (1499-1506). Ed. Injac Zamputi. Tiranë, 1979.

Doukas. *Decline and Fall of Byzantium to the Ottoman Turks.* Trans. Harry J. Magoulios. Detroit: Wayne State University Press, 1975.

Drizari, Nelo. *Scanderbeg: His Life, Correspondence, Orations, Victories, and Philosophy.* Palo Alto, CA, 1968.

Ducellier, Alain. "La façade maritime de la principauté des Kastriote, de la fin du XIVe siècle à la mort de Skanderbeg," in *Studia Albanica,* 5:1 (1968), pp. 119-136.

Ducellier, Alain. *La façade maritime de l'Albanie au Moyen Âge: Durazzo et Valona du XIe au XVe siècle*. Thessaloniki: Institute for Balkan Studies, 1981.

Ducellier, Alain. "The Genesis and Failure of the Albanian State in the Fourteenth and Fifteenth Centuries," pp. 3-22 in *Studies on Kosovo*. Ed. Arshi Pipa and Sami Repishti. New York: East European Monographs, Columbia University Press, 1984.

Durham, Mary Edith. *The Burden of the Balkans*. London, 1905.

Dvorik, Francis. *The Slavs in European History and Civilization*. New Brunswick, NJ: Rutgers University Press, 1962.

East, Gordon. *Géographie historique de l'Europe*. Paris, 1939.

Edmonds, Paul. *To the Land of the Eagle: Travels in Montenegro and Albania*. New York: E.P. Dutton & Co., 1927.

Effendi, Wassa. *Études sur l'Albanie et les Albanais*. Constantinople: Typ. Lith. du Journal «La Turque», 1879.

Encyclopedia of Islam. Eds. H.A.R. Gibb, J.H. Kramers, et.al. Leiden, 1960.

Encyclopedia of Islam. Eds. B. Lewis, Ch. Pellat, and J. Scacht. Leiden, 1965.

Federal Writers' Project of the Works Progress Administration of Massachusetts. *The Albanian Struggle in the Old World and New*. Boston: The Writer Inc., Publishers, 1939.

Fine, John V.A. *The Late Medieval Balkans: A Critical Survey from the Late Twelfth Century to the Ottoman Conquest*. Ann Arbor: University of Michigan Press, 1987.

Fischer-Galati, Stephen. *Man, State, and Society in East European History.* New York: Praeger Publishers, 1970.

Fisher, Sidney. *The Foreign Relations of Turkey, 1481-1512.* Urbana, IL: University of Illinois, 1948.

Fjalor Enciklopedik Shqiptar. Ed. Aleks Buda. Tiranë, 1985.

Fossier, Robert,Ed. *The Cambridge Illustrated History of the Middle Ages, III, 1250-1520.* Trans. Sarah Hanbury Tenison. Cambridge: Cambridge University Press, 1986.

Frashëri, Kristo. *George Kastrioti-Scanderbeg: The National Hero of the Albanians, 1405-1468.* Tirana: State Publishing Enterprise «Naim Frashëri», 1962.

Frashëri, Kristo. *The History of Albania: A Brief Survey.* Tirana, 1964.

Frashëri, Kristo. "Le pays des Albanais au XVe siècle," pp. 127-142 in *Deuxième conference des études albonologiques: à l'occasion du 5e centenaire de la mort de Georges Kastriote-Skanderbeg, Tirana, 12-16 janvier 1968.* Tirana: Université d'état de Tirana, Institut d'histoire et de linguistique, 1969. Volume 1.

Frazee, Charles A. *Catholics and Sultans: The Church and the Ottoman Empire, 1453-1923.* New York and London: Cambridge University Press, 1983.

Gegaj, Athanase. *L'Albanie et l'invasion turque au XVe siècle.* Louvain: Bibliothèque de l'Université, 1937.

Gentleman, Z.I. *The Famous Acts of George Castrioti, Surnamed Scanderbeg, King of the Epirots, Now Named Albanois.* London, 1598.

George Kastriot-Scanderbeg and the Albanian-Turkish War of the XVth Century. Tirana: The State University of Tirana, Institute of History and Linguistics, 1967.

Gibbon, Edward. *The Decline and Fall of the Roman Empire, Volume 3: 1185 A.D.-1453 A.D.* New York: Random House, The Modern Library, 1932.

Gibert, Frédéric. *Les pays d'Albanie et leur histoire.* Paris: Libraire P. Rosier, 1914.

Gjeçov, Shtjefën. *Kanuni i Lekë Dukagjinit / The Code of Lekë Dukagjini.* Trans. Leonard Fox. Forest Hills, NY, 1989.

Guilmartin, John Francis. *Gunpowder and Galleys: Changing Technology and Mediterranean Warfare at Sea in the Sixteenth Century.* London, 1974.

Guthmundsson, Finnabogi. "Scanderbeg in Icelandic Sources," in *Studia Albanica*, 22:1 (1985), pp. 201-208.

Hadri, Flamur. "L'historiographie albanaise sur les sources documentaires et littéraires de l'epoque de Scanderbeg," in *Studia Albanica*, 23:2 (1986), pp. 47-68.

Halecki, Oskar. *From Florence to Brest (1439-1596).* 2nd edition. New York: Archon Books, 1968.

Hammer, J. de. *Histoire de l'Empire Ottoman depuis son origine jusqu'à nos jours. Volume III.* Paris, 1836.

Hammond, N.G.L. *Epirus: The geography, the Ancient Remains, the History, and the Topography of Epirus and Adjacent Areas.* Oxford: Clarendon Press, 1967.

Hasluck, F.W. *Christianity and Islam under the Sultans.* 2 volumes. Ed. Margaret Hasluck. New York: Octagon Books, 1973.

Hasluck, Margaret. *The Unwritten Law in Albania*. Ed. J.H. Hutton. Cambridge: Cambridge University Press, 1954.

Hay, Denys. *Europe in the Fourteenth and Fifteenth Centuries*. 2nd edition. London and New York, 1989.

Held, Joseph. *Hunyadi: Legend and Reality*. New York: East European Monographs, Columbia University Press, 1985.

Hilton, Rodney. *Bond Men Made Free: Medieval Peasant Movements and the English Rising of 1381*. New York: The Viking Press, 1973.

Hilton, Rodney. *Class Conflict and the Crisis of Feudalism: Essays in Medieval Social History*. London: The Hambledon Press, 1985.

Hilton, Rodney. "A Crisis of Feudalism," in *Past and Present*, 80 (August, 1978), pp. 3-19.

Hilton, Rodney. *The Decline of Serfdom in Medieval England*. London: MacMillan & Co., 1969.

Hilton, Rodney and H. Fagan. *The English Rising of 1381*. London: Lawrence and Wishart, 1950.

Hilton, Rodney. "Peasant Society, Peasant Movements, and Feudalism in Medieval Europe," pp. 67-94 in *Rural Protest: Peasant Movements and Social Change*. Ed. Henry A. Landsberger. London: The MacMillan Press Ltd., 1974.

Hilton, Rodney, ed. *The Transition from Feudalism to Capitalism*. London: NLB, 1976.

Hobhouse, J.C. *A Journey through Albania and other Provinces of Turkey in Europe and Asia, to Constantinople, during the Years 1809 and 1810.* London : James Cawthorn, 1813.

Hrabak, Bogumil. "Exportations de céréales de l'Albanie aux XIVe et XVe siècles," in *Studia Albanica*, 5:2 (1968), pp. 111-114.

Hughes, T.S. *Travels in Greece and Albania.* 2 volumes. 2nd edition. London: Henry Colburn and Richard Bentley, 1830.

Imber, Colin. "The Navy of Suleyman the Magnificent," in *Archivum Ottomanicum*, 6 (1980), pp. 211-282.

Inalcik, Halil. "Mehmed the Conqueror and His Time," in *Speculum*, 35:3 (1960), pp. 408- 427.

Inalcik, Halil. *The Ottoman Empire: The Classical Age, 1300-1600.* Trans. Norman Itzkowitz and Colin Imber. New York: Praeger Publishers, 1973.

Inalcik, Halil. "Timariotes chrétiens en Albanie au XVe siècle," pp. 118-138 in *Osterreichisches Staatsarchiv Mitteilungen.* Volume 4. Vienna, 1952.

Iorga, Nicolae. *Brève histoire de l'Albanie et du peuple Albanais.* Bucarest, 1919.

Isaku, Skënder. "L'art militaire de Skanderbeg," in *Studia Albanica*, 5:1 (1968), pp. 169- 176.

Islami, Selim and Kristo Frashëri. *Historia e Popullit Shqiptar.* Volume I. Tiranë, 1967.

Jovius, Paulus. *A Short Treatise upon the Turkes Chronicles, compyled by Paulus Jovius, Bishop of Nucerne and dedicated to Charles the V Emperour.* Trans. Peter Ashton. London: Edwarde Whitchurch, 1546.

Kelly, J.N.D. *The Oxford Dictionary of Popes*. Oxford: Oxford University Press, 1986.

Kemal, Ismail. *The Memoirs of Ismail Kemal Bey*. London: Constable & Co., Ltd., 1920.

Kinross, Lord. *The Ottoman Centuries: The Rise and Fall of the Turkish Empire*. New York: William Morrow & Co., Inc., 1977.

Király, Béla K. "Society and War from Mounted Knights to the Standing Armies of the Absolute Kings: Hungary and the West," pp. 23-55 in *From Hunyadi to Rákóczi: War and Society in Late Medieval and Early Modern Hungary*. Eds. János M. Bak and Béla K. Király. Brooklyn: Brooklyn College Press, 1982.

Knight, Edward F. *Albania: A Narrative of Recent Travel*. London: Sampson Low, Marston, Searle & Rivington, 1880.

Knolles, Richard. *The Generall Historie of the Turkes from the first beginning of that Nation to the rising of the Othoman Familie; with all the notable expeditions of the Christian Princes against them. Together with the Lives and Conquests of the Othoman Kings and Emperours*. 5th edition. London: Adam Islif, 1638.

Konitza, Faik. *Albania: The Rock Garden of Southeastern Europe and Other Essays*. Ed. G.M. Panarity. Boston: VATRA (Pan-Albanian Federation of America), 1957.

Kritovoulos. *History of Mehmed the Conqueror*. Trans. Charles T. Riggs. Princeton: Princeton University Press, 1954.

Kriedte, Peter, Hans Medick, and Jurgen Schlumbohm, eds. *Industrialization before Industrialization: Rural Industry in the Genesis of Capitalism*. Trans. Beate Schempp. Cambridge: Cambridge university Press, 1981.

Kula, Witold. *An Economic theory of the Feudal System: Towards a Model of the Polish Economy, 1500-1800.* Trans. Lawrence Garner. London: NLB, 1976.

Ladurie, Emmanuel LeRoy. *The Peasants of Lanmguedoc.* Trans. John Day. Urbana, IL: University of Illinois Press, 1974.

Lane, Frederic C. *Venice: A Maritime Republic.* Baltimore: Johns Hopkins University Press, 1973.

Leunclavius. *Historia Musulmana Turcorum de monumentis ipsorum exscripta.* 1591.

Langer, William L., ed. *An Encyclopedia of World History: Ancient, Medieval, and Modern, Chronologically Arranged.* Revised edition. Boston: Houghton, Mifflin Co., 1948.

Licho, Edward A., ed. *Gjergj Kastrioti Skënderbeu, 1468-1968.* Boston: VATRA, 1968.

Lis, Catharina and Hugo Soly. *Poverty and Capitalism in Pre-Industrial Europe.* Atlantic Highlands, NJ: Humanities Press, Inc., 1979.

Logoreci, Anton. *The Albanians: Europe's Forgotten Survivors.* London: Victor Gollancz, Ltd., 1977.

Longfellow, Henry Wadsworth. *The Complete Writings of Henry Wadsworth Longfellow.* Volume IV. Boston: Houghton, Mifflin Co., 1904.

Longworth, Philip. *The Making of Eastern Europe.* London: The MacMillan Press, 1992.

Ludlow, James M. *The Captain of the Janizaries: A Story of the Times of Scanderbeg and the Fall of Constantinople.* 11th edition. New York: B.W. Dodge & Co., 1890.

Lufta Shqiptaro-Turke në shekullin XV: Burime osmane. Ed. Selami Pulaha. Tiranë, 1968.

Magno, Stefano. "Évènements historiques en Grèce (1479-1497)," in *Documents inédits relatifs à l'histoire de la Grèce au Moyen Âge*. Volume 6. Ed. D.N. Sathas. Paris, 1884.

Mallett, M.E. and J.R. Hale. *The Military Organization of a Renaissance State: Venice c. 1400 to 1617*. Cambridge: Cambridge University Press, 1984.

Malltezi, Luan. "Le monopole de l'état de Venise sur les céréales en Albanie au XVe siècle," in *Studia Albanica*, 24:1 (1987), pp. 139-160.

Malltezi, Luan. *Qytetet e bregdetit Shqiptar gjatë sundimit Venedikas, 1392-1478*. Tiranë, 1988.

Mann, Stuart E. *Albanian Literature: An Outline of Prose, Poetry, and Drama*. London: Bernard Quaritch Ltd., 1955.

Marinesco, Constantin. "Alphonse V, roi d'Aragon et de Naples, et l'Albanie de Scanderbeg," pp. 7-135 in *Melanges de l'école roumaine en France*. Paris, 1923.

Marmullaku, Ramadan. *Albania and the Albanians*. Trans. Margot and Bosko Milosavljevic. Hamden, CT: Archon Books, 1975.

McNeil, William H. *Venice: The Hinge of Europe, 1081-1797*. Chicago: University of Chicago Press, 1974.

Mehmed, Mustafa Ali. *Istoria Turcilor*. București: Editura Științifică și Enciclopedică, 1976.

Mihailović, Konstantin. *Memoirs of a Janissary*. Trans. Benjamin Stolz. Ed. Svat Soucek. Ann Arbor: The University of Michigan, 1975.

Mijatovich, Chemodil. *Constantine, the Last Emperor of the Greeks, or the Conquest of Constantinople by the Turks.* London: Sampson, Low, Marston & Co., 1892.

Miller, William. *Essays on the Latin Orient.* Cambridge: Cambridge University Press, 1921.

Miller, William. "The Last Athenian Historian: Laonikos Chalkokondyles," in *Journal of Hellenic Studies*, 42 (1922), pp. 36-49.

Moore, Clement C. *George Castriot, Surnamed Scanderbeg, King of Albania.* New York: D. Appleton & Co., 1850.

Mosely, Philip E. "The Peasant Family: The Zadruga, or Communal Joint-Family in the Balkans and its Recent Development," pp. 95-108 in *The Cultural Approach to History.* Ed. Caroline F. Ware. New York: Columbia University Press, 1940.

Moutafchieva, Vera P. *Agrarian Relations in the Ottoman Empire in the 15th and 16th Centuries.* New York: East European Monographs, Columbia University Press, 1988.

Mureşan, Camil. *Iancu de Hunedoara.* 2nd edition. Bucureşti, 1968.

Myrdal, Jan and Gun Kessle. *Albania Defiant.* Trans. Paul Britten Austin. New York: Monthly Review Press, 1976.

Naçi, Stavri N. "A propos de quelques truchements concernant les rapports de la papauté avec Skanderbeg, durant la lutte albano-turque (1443-1468)," in *Studia Albanica*, 5:1 (1968), pp. 73-86.

Nicol, Donald M. *The Despotate of Epiros, 1267-1479: A Contribution to the History of Greece in the Middle Ages.* Cambridge: Cambridge University Press, 1984.

Nicol, Donald M. *The End of the Byzantine Empire.* London: Edward Arnold Publishers, Ltd., 1979.

Noli, Fan Stylian. *George Castrioti Scanderbeg (1405-1468).* New York: International Universities Press, 1947.

Ostrogorsky, George. *History of the Byzantine State.* Trans. Joan Hussey. New Brunswick: Rutgers University Press, 1957.

Paganel, Camille. *Histoire de Scanderbeg ou Turks et Chrétiens au XVe siècle.* Paris: Libraire-Éditeur, 1855.

Pall, Francisc. *Marino Barlezio: Uno storico umanista.* Bucuresti, 1938.

Pall, Francisc. "Une nouvelle histoire de Scanderbeg: remarques sur le livre de M. Gegaj," in *Revue historique du sud-est européen*, 14:10-12 (1937), pp. 293-306.

Pall, Francisc. "Les relations entre la Hongrie et Scanderbeg," in *Revue historique du sud-est européen*, 10:4-6 (1933), pp. 119-141.

Pall, Francisc. "Skanderbeg et Janco de Hunedoara (Jean Hunyadi)," in *Studia Albanica*, 5:1 (1968), pp. 103-118.

Pano, Nicholas C. *The People's Republic of Albania.* Baltimore: The Johns Hopkins Press, 1968.

Parker, Geoffrey. *The Military Revolution: Military Innovation and the rise of the West, 1500-1800.* Cambridge: Cambridge University Press, 1988.

Pastor, Ludwig. *The History of the Popes from the Close of the Middle Ages*. Ed. Frederick Ignatius Antrobus. Volume II, London: John Hodges, 1891; Volume III, London: Routledge and Kegan Paul, Ltd., 1949; Volume IV, London: Kegan Paul, Trench, Trübner & Co., 1894.

Petrovic, Djurdjica. "Fire-arms in the Balkans on the Eve of and After the Ottoman Conquests of the Fourteenth and Fifteenth Centuries," pp. 164-194 in *War, Technology, and Society in the Middle East*. Eds. V.J. Parry and M.E. Yapp. London: Oxford University Press, 1975.

Pétrovitch, Georges T. *Scanderbeg (Georges Castriota): Essai de bibliographie raisonnée. Ouvrages sur Scanderbeg écrits en langues française, anglaise, allemande, latine, italienne, espagnole, portugaise, suédoise et greque et publiés depuis l'invention de l'imprimerie jusqu'à nos jours*. Paris: Ernest Leroux, éditeur, 1881.

Pirenne, Henri. *Social and Economic History of Medieval Europe*. New York: Harcourt, Brace & World, Inc., n.d.

Pisko, Julius. *Skanderbeg. Historische Studie*. Wien: K.V.K. Hofbuchhandlung Wilhelm Frick, 1894.

Pitcher, Donald Edgar. *An Historical Geography of the Ottoman Empire from the Earliest Times to the End of the Sixteenth Century*. Leiden: E.J. Brill, 1972.

Pius II. "The Commentaries of Pius II," trans. Florence Alden Gragg, in *Smith College Studies in History*: Books II and III, 25:1-4 (October, 1939-July, 1940); Books VI- IX, 35 (1951); Books X-XIII, 43 (1957). Northhampton, MA.

Pollo, Stefanaq and Arben Puto. *The History of Albania from its Origins to the Present Day*. Trans. Carol Wiseman and Ginnie Hole. London: Routledge & Kegan Paul, 1981.

Pollo, Stefanaq, ed. *Historia e Shqipërisë*. Volume II. Tiranë, 1984.

Pontieri, Ernesto. *Ferrante d'Aragona re di Napoli*. Napoli, 1969.

Postan, M.M. *The Medieval Economy and Society: An Economic History of Britain*. Berkeley: University of California Press, 1972.

Presurtare din istoria lui Gheorghe Kastriotul numit Skenderbei, prințul Albaniei. Trans. I. Bilcirescu. Bucuresci, 1847.

Prifti, Peter R. *Socialist Albania since 1944: Domestic and Foreign Developments*. Cambridge, MA: MIT Press, 1978.

Pulaha, Selami. "Aspectes de demographie historique des contrées albanaises pendant les XVe-XVIe siècles," in *Studia Albanica*, 21:2 (1984), pp. 65-76.

Pulaha, Selami. "Les Kastriote devant la conquête ottomane des années, 1420-1430," in *Studia Albanica*, 8:1 (1971), pp. 103-128.

Pulaha, Selami. *On the Demographic and Ethnical Situation of the Albanian Territories (15th-16th Centuries)*. Tirana, 1988.

Pulaha, Selami, ed. *Lufta Shqiptaro-Turke në shekullin XV: Burime Osmane*. Tiranë, 1968.

Pulaha, Selami. *Pronësia feudale në tokat Shqiptare, shek. XV-XVI*. Tiranë, 1988.

Radonić, Jovan. *Gjuradj Kastrioti Skenderbeg i Arbanija u XV veku*. Beograd, 1942.

Radeshi, Dilaver. *Beteja e Drinit dhe Oranikut*. Tiranë, 1964.

Ranke, Leopold von. *Sämmtliche Werke: Serbien und die Türkei*. Volume 44. Leipzig, 1879.

Rapo, Aleko. "La lutte des Himariotes, partie intégrante de la lutte des Albanais pour la liberté et l'indépendence au XV-début du XVIe siècles," pp. 275-281 in *Deuxième conference des études albanologiques: à l'occasion du 5e centenaire de la mort de Georges Kastriote-Skanderbeg, Tirana, 12-16 janvier 1968*. Volume I. Tirana: Université d'état de Tirana, Institut d'histoire et de linguistique, 1969.

Runciman, Steven. *The Fall of Constantinople, 1453*. Cambridge: Cambridge University Press, 1965.

Ryder, Alan. *The Kingdom of Naples under Alphonso the Magnanimous: The Making of a Modern State*. Oxford: Clarendon Press, 1976.

Sardella, Pierre. *Nouvelles et spéculations à Venise au début du XVIe siècle*. Paris, 1948.

Schevill, Ferdinand. *History of the Balkan Peninsula: From the Earliest Times to the Present Day*. New York: Frederick Ungar Publishing, 1966.

Schwoebel. *The Shadow of the Crescent: The Renaissance Image of the Turk (1453- 1517)*. New York, 1967.

Setton, Kenneth M., ed. *A History of the Crusades, Volume II: The Later Crusades, 1189- 1311*. Madison: University of Wisconsin Press, 1969.

Setton, Kenneth M., ed. *A History of the Crusades, Volume III: The Fourteenth and Fifteenth Centuries*. Madison: University of Wisconsin Press, 1975.

Setton, Kenneth M. *The Papacy and the Levant (1204-1571), Volume II: The Fifteenth Century*. Philadelphia: The American Philosophical Society, 1978.

Shaw, George Bernard. *Four Plays by Bernard Shaw*. New York, 1965.

Shaw, Stanford J. *History of the Ottoman Empire and Modern Turkey, Volume I: The Empire of the Gazis. The Rise and Decline of the Ottoman Empire, 1280-1808*. New York: Cambridge University Press, 1976.

Shelley, Percy Bysshe. *Shelley, Poetical Works*. Ed. Thomas Hutchinson. Oxford: Oxford University Press, 1991.

Shuteriqi, Dhimitër S. "Les relations entre Skanderbeg et georges Aranite dans les années 1449-1450," pp. 105-116 in *Deuxième conference des études albanologiques: à l'occasion du 5e centenaire de la mort de Georges Kastriote-Skanderbeg, Tirana, 12-16 janvier 1968*. Tirana: Université d'état de Tirana, Institut d'histoire et de linguistique, 1969.

Simonde de Sismondi, Jean Charles Leonard. *Histoire des Républiques Italiennes du Moyen Âge*. Volume 7. Paris, 1840.

Simonde de Sismondi, Jean Charles Leonard. *A History of the Italian Republics: Being a View of the origin, Progress, and Fall of Italian Freedom*. Abridged edition. Garden City, NY: Anchor Books, Doubleday & Co., Inc., 1966.

Skendi, Stavro. *Albania*. New York: Frederick A. Praeger, 1958.

Skendi, Stavro. *The Albanian National Awakening, 1878-1912.* Princeton: Princeton University Press, 1967.

Skendi, Stavro. "The Complex Environment of Skenderbeg's Activity," pp. 167-186 in *Balkan Cultural Studies.* New York: East European Monographs, Columbia University Press, 1980.

Skendi, Stavro. "Religion in Albania during Ottoman Rule," in *Südost-Forschungen*, 15 (1986), pp. 311-327.

Skendi, Stavro. "Skenderbeg and the Albanian National Consciousness," pp. 205-210 in *Balkan Cultural Studies.* New York: East European Monographs, Columbia University Press, 1980.

Sphrantzes, George. *The Fall of the Byzantine Empire.* Trans. Marios Philippides. Amherst: The University of Massachusetts Press, 1980.

Spinka, Matthew. *A History of Christianity in the Balkans: A Study in the Spread of Byzantine Culture among the Slavs.* Chicago: American Society of Church History, 1933.

Stavrianos, L.S. *The Balkans since 1453.* New York: Holt, Rinehart and Winston, 1958.

Stavrou, M.S. *Études sur l'Albanie.* Paris: Éditions de "La vie universitaire," 1922.

Stevenson, Francis Seymour. *A History of Montenegro.* London, 1912; Reprint, New York: Arno Press and the New York Times, 1971.

Stoianovich, Traian. *A Study in Balkan Civilization.* New York: Alfred A. Knopf, 1967.

Strabo. *The Geography of Strabo*. Vol. III. Trans. Horace Leonard Jones. Cambridge, MA: Harvard University Press, 1960.

Studime për epokën e Skënderbeut. 3 Vols. Tiranë, 1989.

Sugar, Peter. *A History of East Central Europe, Volume V: Southeastern Europe under Ottoman Rule, 1354-1804*. Seattle and London: University of Washington Press, 1977.

Swinburne, Henry. *Travels in the Two Sicilies in the Years 1777, 1778, 1779, and 1780*. 2 volumes. London: P. Elmsly, 1783.

Swire, Joseph. *Albania: The Rise of a Kingdom*. London: Williams & Norgate Ltd., 1929.

Thiriet, Freddy. "Quelques réflexions sur la politique Vénitienne à l'égard de Georges Skanderbeg," in *Studia Albanica*, 5:1 (1968), pp. 87-94.

Thomson, John A.F. *Popes and Princes, 1417-1517: Politics and Polity in the Late Medieval Church*. London: George Allen & Unwin, 1980.

Thuasne, L. *Djem-Sultan, fils de Mohammed II, frère de Bayezid II (1459-1495)*. Paris, 1892.

Thucydides. *The Pelopponnesian War*. Trans. Rex Warner. Harmondsworth: Penguin Books, 1985.

Tihany, Leslie C. *A History of Middle Europe: From the Earliest Times to the Age of the World Wars*. New Brunswick: Rutgers University Press, 1976.

Treptow, Kurt W. "Albania and the Ottoman Invasion of Italy, 1480-1481," in *Studia Albanica*, 27:1 (1990), pp. 81-105.

Treptow, Kurt W. "Distance and Communications in South-eastern Europe, 1593-1612," in *East European Quarterly*, 24:4 (Winter, 1990), pp. 475-482.

Treptow, Kurt W. "The Formation of the Albanian National Consciousness," in *The Ukrainian Quarterly*, 48:4 (Winter, 1992), pp. 437-467.

Treptow, Kurt W. *From Zalmoxis to Jan Palach: Studies in East European History*. New York: East European Monographs, Columbia University Press, 1992.

Treptow, Kurt W. "The Ottoman Invasion of Italy and the Albanian Rebellion, 1480-1481," in *The Ukrainian Quarterly*, 47:1 (Spring, 1991), pp. 54-72; continued in *The Ukrainian Quarterly*, 47:2 (Summer, 1991), pp. 182-190.

Treptow, Kurt W. "The Role of Religion in the Development of the Albanian Nation- State: From the Rise of National Consciousness to the Fall of National Communism," in *The Ukrainian Quarterly* (1995).

Tuleja, Thaddeus V. "Eugenius IV and the Crusade of Varna," in *Catholic Historical Review*, 35:3 (October, 1949), pp. 257-275.

Tursun Beg. *The History of Mehmed the Conqueror*. Trans. Halil Inalcik and Rhoads Murphey. Minneapolis and Chicago: Bibliotheca Islamica, 1978.

Vaughan, Dorothy M. *Europe and the Turk: A Pattern of Alliances, 1350-1700*. Liverpool: University Press, 1954.

Vaughan, Richard. *Philip the Good: The Apogee of Burgundy*. New York: Barnes & Noble, 1973.

Vucinich, Wayne S. "The Nature of Balkan Society under Ottoman Rule," in *Slavic Review*, 21:4 (June, 1962), pp. 597-616.

Ware, Timothy. *The Orthodox Church*. Harmondsworth: Penguin Books, 1985.

Willson, Beckles. *The Life and Letters of James Wolfe*. New York: Dodd, Mead & Co., 1909.

Zamputi, Injac. "I biri i Skënderbeut — Gjon Kartioti dhe lëvizja e armatosur në Shqipëri më 1481: Dokumenta dhe materiale," in *Zëri i rinise*, 12 gusht 1967, pp. 3-4.

HISTRIA BOOKS

ALSO AVAILABLE:

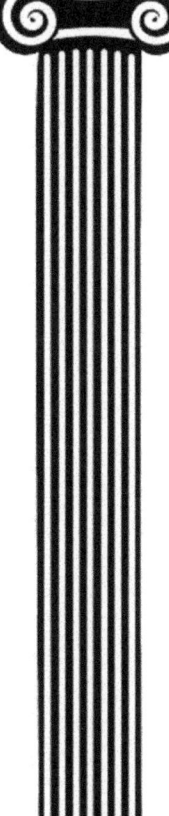

HISTRIABOOKS.COM

Lightning Source UK Ltd.
Milton Keynes UK
UKHW011814280519

343474UK00001B/120/P